Taking Sides

Speaking Skills for College Students

SECOND EDITION

Kevin B. King

Ann Arbor
The University of Michigan Press

Published in the United States of America by
The University of Michigan Press
Manufactured in the United States of America
♾ Printed on acid-free paper

ISBN 978-0-472-03297-6   £21·25

2011   2010   2009   2008   4   3   2   1

Illustrated by William H. Bonney.

This book is for my son, Aidan Wolff-King.

Acknowledgments

Grateful acknowledgment is made to the following authors, publishers, and individuals for permission to reprint previously published materials.

The National Court Reporters' Association for permission to use the 26 pieces in the *Humor in the Court* section (Unit 3) from the book *More Humor in the Court*, edited by Mary Louise Gilman (Vienna, VA: National Court Reporters' Association, 1984).

The New York Times Company for excerpt from "The Solvable Problem of Organ Shortages" by Jane E. Brody. ©2007. Reprinted with permission.

Reuters for the article "Why Japanese Gourmands Will Die for a Taste of Fugu," January 28, 1992. Reuters/Susume Takahaski/Archive Photos for photo of tiger blowfish.

Sage Publications for many of the questions in the *Marital Issues* section (which appears in Unit 5), which derive from Mary Ann Fitzpatrick's book, *Between Husbands and Wives* (Thousand Oaks, CA: 1984). Copyright © 1984. Reprinted by permission of Sage Publications, Inc.

The sections *The Desert Dilemma* (Unit 4) and *Synergy (Lost at Sea)* (Unit 1) have been adapted from photocopied material in circulation more than two decades ago, the provenance of which has proved untraceable.

Experiments 5 and 6 in *Rationality (Sunk Costs)* were adapted from an example created by Amos Tversky and Daniel Kahneman from "The Framing of Decisions and the Psychology of Choice," *Science* 211:453–458 (1981). Reprinted with permission from AAAS.

Experiments 2, 3, and 4 in *Rationality (Sunk Costs)* were adapted from material created by Hal Arkes and Catherine Blumer in "The Psychology of Sunk Costs," *Organizational Behavior and Human Decision Processes* 35 (1985) and published by Academic Press, Orlando, FL.

Every effort has been made to contact the copyright holders for permission to reprint borrowed material. We regret any oversights that may have occurred and will rectify them in future printings.

Contents

To the Student

The speaking exercises in this text allow you to discuss and debate a wide variety of serious topics. These are of general interest; however, they will also prepare you for many of the issues you will discuss or write about as you attend college. There is a lot of new vocabulary, and the most difficult words (which will appear in bold) appear in the Vocabulary Gloss sections. Many of the activities include writing assignments.

Although many of the new vocabulary words are defined for you, you will undoubtedly find some that you do not know. When this occurs, ask other students the meanings of these words. Use this opportunity to teach each other. If possible, use the context to help understand unknown words. The section on **Coercion/Paternalism** (pages 53–62) shows you how to do this.

In each section you will be asked questions that are designed to stimulate differences of opinion. In most cases, there is no answer that is clearly the right one. You can learn as much from one another as you can from simply listening to a teacher's opinion on an issue.

By doing the exercises included in each section, you will improve your problem-solving and critical-thinking abilities. You will also improve your negotiating skills and learn some concepts that are entirely new. You will learn to articulate your opinions on concepts you already know. You will learn a lot about American culture and about how it might differ from yours. You will learn something about the cultures of your classmates as well, especially in The International View sections, where you consider the topics entirely from your own perspective, taking the discussion in any direction you want.

You will also learn many **Conversation Cues.** These are words or phrases that we regularly use for speech functions like interrupting or disagreeing. Knowing some of these will make your conversation flow more smoothly and sound more like the conversation of a native speaker.

With a few exceptions, each unit should be prepared at home, before class. You will make your personal decision on an issue or issues, and then you will share your decision with the class in general or with small groups of students. Finally, you will enjoy engaging in the debates that the exercises in this book will stimulate.

To get into college, many of you will have to take the TOEFL® iBT, which includes a speaking section with two tasks; you will practice each in the chapters of this book. In the independent speaking task, you will be asked questions about familiar topics and will respond using personal knowledge. In the integrated speaking task, you will read a short passage and then hear a short passage. Taking notes on both, you will have a short time to prepare a response that incorporates both listening and reading notes.

Strategies for Speaking Sections of TOEFL®

You will sometimes be asked to **summarize.** Here are a few handy summarizing phrases that you can memorize and use.

1. *The crux of the issue is* _____.
   (crux *means most important, crucial, point*)

2. *What this all boils down to is* _____.

3. *The issue at hand is, basically,* _____.

4. *What the speaker is saying, essentially, is* _____.

5. *What this question is asking, basically, is* _____.

6. *What the* passage *is telling us is, essentially,* _____.
   paragraph

You will also be asked to **present both sides** of an issue or a plan, its advantages and disadvantages. For these cases it can help to have an organizational structure in mind because one of the criteria for judging your score is coherency.

There are pros and cons to the issue of _____.

The pros include _____.

The cons include _____.

On the whole, I favor _____.

   or

On the whole, I'm inclined to side with those who think that _____.

You could memorize this or prepare your own organizational framework for such a speech.

Being silent is the worst thing you can do on a speaking test. You need to be prepared if you do not know what else to say. If you know that you are leaving a long block of silence, you have two options: repetition and circumlocution. Both are better than silence.

Repetition

Use one of these phrases, and then say what you already have said.

1. *Let me make perfectly clear what I am saying here:*

2. *In a nutshell, that's what I am saying. To make this perfectly clear, let me reiterate*

> *my main points:*
>
> *my main arguments:*
>
> *the gist of what I've been saying:*
>
> *the points I've been trying to get across:*

Circumlocution

This means talking around a subject, not coming directly to a point. It's filling in the empty spaces with words. Repetition is probably a better strategy for dealing with large gaps of silence, but what do you do when you have little to repeat because you don't understand a subject? You circumlocute. It is best if you create and memorize your own circumlocutions, but here is an example to give you an idea.

> *It is not clear to me that I have anything prescient to say about _____. In fact, it strikes me as a pretty boring topic. I wish the test-designers had come up with something more interesting.*

Praise the Messenger

Secretary General of the United Nations Ban Ki Moon, a former student of mine at the Kennedy School of Government at Harvard University, used to laugh at how often teachers would say, "Good question" in response to student queries. Indeed, it is another old rhetorical trick to **praise the messenger** when you don't have much to say about the message. The tact is often advisable even when you do have something to say about the message. It can never hurt to praise the intelligence of a question. Here are a couple of phrases you can use to begin your response:

> *The question is a fascinating one.*
> *a multifaceted one.*
> *an intriguing one.*

Or put two together:

> *The question is a fascinating and multifaceted one.*

Such a beginning shows that you know something about rhetoric and shows some good vocabulary knowledge. You might think of an introductory sentence of your own.

What's New in This Edition?

The most significant change in the second edition is the addition of a great amount of material aimed at helping students prepare for the speaking section of the iBT. Each unit has exercises based on the independent speaking task and the integrated speaking task.

Two newspaper articles have been replaced with updated ones on the subject of marriage and Internet material, not available for the first edition, has been incorporated. Further, the dilemma of organ transplantation is addressed because it is so frequently in the news, and the ethical and practical aspects of the issue have been addressed in new ways, which allow for strong argumentation on both sides.

The section on Synergy (Lost at Sea) has been moved to the first unit for two reasons: First, the topic doesn't fit neatly into any of the academic disciplines of the subsequent units and, second, because it is easy and a student favorite.

The psychology unit has been moved from Unit 2 to Unit 5 because it is a little more difficult than the material that now precedes it. However, teachers are encouraged to pick the units they do in whatever order seems best for them. If they have a strong interest in psychology, then that unit can be done earlier.

The business negotiation unit now precedes the linguistics unit (the last two units) because, based on my experience, students tend to be more interested in business and because the linguistics unit is a bit more difficult.

Introductory Exercises

Roommate Search

What are the most important characteristics for assessing the compatibility of a roommate?

Objectives

- to get to know your fellow students and their values better

- to see that different opinions on the same subject are valid and to be tolerated

- to practice the arts of compromise and consensus reaching

- to understand better your own priorities in finding a roommate

- to practice the skill of interviewing potential roommates

- to practice *Conversation Cues* for *Stating Opinions* and *Suggestion*

Introduction

If you study away from home, you will probably find yourself in the situation of trying to find a roommate to share the cost of an apartment. What are the most important characteristics for assessing the **compatibility** of a roommate? We will try to reach a consensus on this question. A *consensus* is a general agreement that not everyone will be in love with but that is a result of negotiation and compromise—it is the best decision that everyone can partially agree on. (Throughout this book, definitions of the words that appear in bold will appear in the Vocabulary Gloss sections.)

Procedure

Part 1

Assume that you are single and are looking for one person to share a two-bedroom apartment. As a class, you will make suggestions for questions that you would ask a potential roommate. The teacher will then write each question as a category on the board. For example, if you would ask, "Do you smoke?" the teacher would write: *smoking*. When you have compiled a list of 12 to 15 items, look at the list and suggest omitting the least important or those that seem to be redundant. You will end up with a list of 10 items. A chart labeled *Roommate Search: Categories and Ranking* follows. Copy the 10 items into the *Category* column of the chart.

Now, individually, you will rank the categories of questions according to their importance: (1) is the most important, (2) is the second most important, and so on, through (10), which is the least important. In other words, if you could ask only one question, which would it be? If it is, "Do you smoke?" then put the number 1 to the right of "Smoking" in the *Personal Ranking* column. If your most important question is, "Could you describe your **lifestyle?**" then put the number 1 to the right of "Lifestyle."

Next, you will meet in groups of three or four to make a consensus ranking. That means that the group as a whole must agree on the ranking. Put 1, 2, etc., for the group decision into the *Group Ranking* column.

Vocabulary Gloss

compatibility = getting along in a friendly manner

lifestyle = this includes things like having parties, having friends over, and preference for loud or soft music

Roommate Search: Categories and Ranking

Category	Personal Ranking	Group Ranking

Part 2

In different groups of four, three students will play the roles of roommates looking for a fourth roommate to take the place of one who just went back to France. You will decide who plays the fourth role—the potential roommate. Ask this person questions to determine whether he or she would be a suitable roommate. When you are done, report to the class as a whole about whether or not you found the student compatible.

Conversation Cues: Stating Opinions, Suggestion

Conversation cues are words or phrases that we regularly use for speech functions such as *interrupting, adding information, disagreeing,* and so forth. If these speech functions are our communicative strategies, then the *conversation cues* are the tactics that we use to accomplish these strategies. Using some of these conversation cues will make your conversation proceed more smoothly and sound more like the conversation of a native speaker. In this unit, we will concentrate on cues for stating opinions and for suggestion. The list of cues will be short, and you already know some, if not many, of them, so we will concentrate on those that are either idiomatic or used very frequently. Using these cues is not the primary focus of the unit, and you should not let the use of them interfere with your normal conversation. Further, the use of these conversation cues should not be limited to this particular unit. Use them now whenever you speak English. You should not feel obligated to use all of them during your discussion, but you should either keep your book open to this page or write the cues on a separate piece of paper and then put a check mark next to a cue each time you use it. At the end of the discussion the teacher will ask you how many times you used these cues. You might be the day's "cue champion."

Stating Opinions

Use these to begin your opinion.

> *Basically,* . . .
> *To my mind,* . . .
> *As far as I can tell,* . . .
> *I'm afraid that,* . . .
> *By and large,* . . .
> *As a rule,* . . .

Usage Notes

Basically is a very popular expression. People use it to refer to the heart of an issue.

> Example: *Basically,* what you are saying is that a woman will never be elected as president, right?

I'm afraid that is also very common and really does not have anything to do with fear. It is just a polite way to begin.

> Example: *I'm afraid that* I don't follow you.

By and large and *as a rule* refer to the general case.

> Example: *By and large,* students prefer open book exams to essay tests. And *as a rule,* students who prepare thoroughly perform better on tests than students who do not read the course materials.

Suggestion

How about . . .

> Examples: *How about* getting a new roommate?
>
> *How about* this: we ask for a rent reduction.

▐▐▶ iBT Preparation

Independent Speaking Task

Students sit in two rows, facing each other. The teacher will read the task. One row will be the speakers (roommate candidates), and the other will be the listeners (interviewers). The speakers will have 15 to 30 seconds (teacher will decide time allotment) to prepare a response of 45 to 60 seconds. When finished, speakers move to the desk immediately to the left and repeat the exercise with a new partner. When speakers have completed the task twice, they become the listeners, so that each student can speak twice. The second time speakers (candidates) give their responses, there will be no preparation time.

Integrated Speaking Task

Read the following passage, and then listen to the passage that the teacher will read. Take notes on both. The teacher will also read a question. You will have 30 seconds to prepare your response. Again, speakers and listeners are in two rows. This time, the speakers respond only once, and then roles are switched.

"Are you a boy, or are you a girl," went a song in the 1960s, when boys started letting their hair grow long, like the Beatles. The question raises problems for college administrators in the 21st century when dealing with transgendered students. Almost all colleges recognize the legitimacy of the claims of these students—that they have bodies of one gender and psyches of the other gender. The question is: Which dorm should they be put in, the boys' or the girls'? And if the college has mixed-gender dorms, should transgendered students be on the floor with the boys or with the girls?

The International View

Discuss the concept of "roommates" in your country. Here are some sample questions to help you begin your discussion.

- Do people tend to live at home and not have roommates?

- What considerations, besides the ones in the list that you used earlier, would be important for finding a suitable roommate in your country?

Synergy (Lost at Sea)

Objectives

- to introduce the concept of synergy

- to understand group dynamics

- to understand that you can learn from your colleagues, as opposed to having knowledge poured into your heads by a teacher

- to practice using *Conversation Cues* for *Changing Your Mind, Asking for Repetition,* and *Interruption*

Introduction

This is an exercise in group decision making. More specifically, it is an exercise in synergy. Synergy is the concept that "two heads are better than one." In other words, when considering an issue, a group of people should be able to make a better decision than any individual in the group. We will test this concept.

Native speakers usually experience synergy in group discussion. Students who are learning another language often do not achieve synergy. There are two major reasons for this. One is that students who do very well individually may be shy and will not try to persuade the others of their opinions. The other is that some students who do not do well individually may love to talk and may be very forceful. Thus, you should be sure to get all of your group members to share the reasons for their choices and avoid letting any one student dominate your discussion.

Vocabulary Gloss

yacht	=	luxurious boat
life raft	=	small emergency boat that you inflate with air
oars	=	long, wooden instruments used to move a boat or raft
crew	=	people who work on a boat
sextant	=	navigational device for use with stars
seat cushion	=	comfortable thing to sit on, like on an airplane
shark repellent	=	liquid that should make sharks go away
20 square feet	=	5 feet high by 4 feet long
opaque	=	blocking the passage of light; can't be seen through
fishing kit	=	little box with the essentials for fishing
wilderness	=	large area of undeveloped land

Lost at Sea

As a consequence of a fire of unknown origin, your **yacht** is slowly sinking in the South Pacific. Your location is unclear because the fire destroyed much of the navigational equipment. Your best estimate is that you're approximately 1,000 miles southwest of the nearest land.

Below is a list of 15 items that are undamaged after the fire. In addition to these articles, you have a rubber **life raft** with **oars** that is large enough to carry yourself and the four **crew** members and all of the items listed. Along with these, you have in your collective pockets one package of cigarettes, several books of matches, and five one-dollar bills.

Part 1: Procedure

Rank the 15 items in terms of their importance to your survival. Place the number 1 by the most important item, the number 2 by the second most important, and so on through number 15, the least important. Ask the class if you don't understand any of the items.

_____ **sextant**

_____ shaving mirror

_____ five-gallon can of water

_____ mosquito netting

_____ one case (24 cans) emergency food

_____ maps of the Pacific Ocean

_____ **seat cushion** (flotation device)

_____ two-gallon can of oil-gas mixture

_____ one battery-powered radio

_____ **shark repellent**

_____ **20 square feet** of **opaque** plastic

_____ one quart of strong rum, 80% alcohol

_____ 15 feet of nylon rope

_____ two boxes of chocolate bars

_____ **fishing kit**

Part 2: Procedure

Use the *Individual/Consensus* ranking sheet on page 11.

1. Copy your own ranking for each item into the column labeled *Repeat Individual*.

2. Now work in groups of three or four. Discuss your individual rankings in whatever way you think best and come up with a consensus about a group ranking. If you cannot get a majority, say 2 to 1, then do not force the minority member to accept your solution: Instead, you must try to convince him or her that your decision is best. You must find a solution that everyone can accept, even if no one person thinks that it is best. You should consider differences of opinion as a help rather than a hindrance in achieving your goal. Find out why the other person chose what he or she did. One way to start is to say, "Okay, what did you put for number one?" At some point, you could work from the bottom (15) up. Write the ranking of the group in the column marked *Group Consensus*.

3. The teacher will read you the best ranking, as decided by officers of the U.S. Merchant Marines. You may not agree with the rationale for these choices, but we must accept it.

4. Write the correct ranking in the appropriate column.

5. Find the difference between your individual ranking and the correct ranking, and put that on the same line as your own individual ranking, to the right of your ranking. It doesn't matter if the difference is a positive (+) or negative (−) number. Just use the number; ignore any minus (−) sign.

6. Find the difference between the group consensus and the correct ranking. Put this number on the same line as the *Group Consensus* ranking. Again, it doesn't matter if it is a positive or a negative number. Just use the number.

7. Total the scores for *Individual* and *Group Consensus*.

(Hypothetical Example)

Correct	Repeat Individual		Group Consensus	
3	1	(2)	7	(4)

You chose 1. Therefore, your score is *2* [the difference between 3 and 1]. The group chose 7. The group score is *4* [the difference between 3 and 7]. Note that the best score is the lowest. A perfect score would be zero.

Correct	Repeat Individual	Group Consensus	
_____	_____	_____	sextant
_____	_____	_____	shaving mirror
_____	_____	_____	five-gallon can of water
_____	_____	_____	mosquito netting
_____	_____	_____	one case (24 cans) emergency food
_____	_____	_____	maps of the Pacific Ocean
_____	_____	_____	seat cushion (flotation device)
_____	_____	_____	two-gallon can of oil-gas mixture
_____	_____	_____	one battery-powered radio
_____	_____	_____	shark repellent
_____	_____	_____	20 square feet of opaque plastic
_____	_____	_____	one quart of strong rum, 80% alcohol (that is, 160 proof)
_____	_____	_____	15 feet of nylon rope
_____	_____	_____	two boxes of chocolate bars
_____	_____	_____	fishing kit
	_____	_____	*(Total)*

Synergy Analysis

After the teacher quickly records individual scores (without names) and the group scores, he or she will give the data to one student who will fill in the following tables and report the results to the class. Synergy is defined as a consensus score lower than the lowest individual score in the group.

	Before Group Discussion	
Group Number	**Average Individual Score in the Group**	**Most Accurate Individual Score in the Group**
Example	55	45
1		
2		
3		
4		
	Average Individual Score for All Groups _____	Most Accurate Individual Score Averaged across All Groups _____

	After Group Discussion			
Group Number	*Score for Group Consensus*	*Gain/Loss over Average Individual*	*Gain/Loss over Most Accurate Individual*	*Synergy (yes/no)*
Example	40	+15°	+5	Yes
1				
2				
3				
4				
Average				

°+15 means that this consensus score was 15 better than the individual score, even though it was 15 lower. Remember, the lower the score, the better it is. A minus (−) would indicate that the consensus score was worse, that is, a larger number.

Conclusion

Discuss why some groups achieved synergy and others did not. Discuss what behaviors helped or hindered the consensus-seeking process.

Conversation Cues

Keep your book open to this page or write the cues on a separate piece of paper. Put a check mark next to a cue each time you use it.

Changing Your Mind

> *On second thought, . . .*

Asking for Repetition

> *I didn't catch that. Could you repeat that?*

Interruption

> *I'd like to jump in.*
> *Can I jump in?*
> *Let me jump in here.*
> *Can I just say that . . .*
> *Can I get my two cents in?*
> *I'd like to get my two cents in, if you don't mind.*

The International View

Can you think of any incidents in your personal experience where "two heads have been better than one"? Or were you ever involved in an incident where synergy was counterproductive—where "two heads were worse than one"?

⫸ iBT Preparation

Independent Speaking Task

Students sit in two rows, facing each other. The teacher will read the task. One row will be the speakers, and the other will be the listeners. The speakers will have 15 to 30 seconds (teacher will decide time allotment) to prepare a response of 45 to 60 seconds. When finished, speakers move to the desk immediately to the left and repeat the exercise with a new partner. When speakers have completed the task twice, they become the listeners, so that each student can speak twice. The second time speakers give their responses, there will be no preparation time.

Integrated Speaking Task

Read the following passage, and then listen to the passage that the teacher will read. Take notes on both. The teacher will also read a question. You will have 30 seconds to prepare your response. Again, speakers and listeners are in two rows. This time, the speakers respond only once, and then roles are switched.

> *There are numerous schools in the United States and around the globe where people are taught how to survive in the* **wilderness**. *You can take a two-day course or a month-long one. Often, you will have to survive by yourself with only a knife, a water bottle, and a tiny survival kit. Things like tents and sleeping bags are forbidden. But it can be dangerous; one person died in a survival school.*

Philosophy (Distributive Justice)

The Candy Bar Dilemma

Objectives

- to develop debating skills

- to create an argument

- to listen to and counter other arguments

- to write from a strong thesis

- to understand and employ the principle of *charity* in persuasive writing and oral argument

Introduction

This apparently simple exercise is a microcosm of issues in distributive justice, a subject that has become increasingly popular in philosophy. Distributive justice examines fairness in holdings—how do we justify having those things we have? This subject is different from *criminal justice,* which is the focus of Unit 3.

First, what comes to your mind when you think about the term *distributive justice?* Is this an issue that has special significance in your country?

Vocabulary Gloss

propensity   = natural tendency

break out in zits = to develop pimples (little spots, generally
                         on the face and sometimes associated
                         with eating sweets)

obese   = extremely fat

arbiter   = judge

The Candy Bar Dilemma

On the table is one candy bar. Three teenagers want it. Andrew has a **propensity** to **break out in zits.** Betty is **obese**. Carol is normal in all respects, but she has just eaten three candy bars. You must distribute the candy bar justly. How will you do it?

On the table is a candy bar. Three teenagers want it.

Procedure

Part 1: How the Candy Bar Should Be Distributed Justly

Discuss the possibilities as a class. Be sure to suggest all reasonable possibilities of distribution (you can divide it or give it wholly). Give reasons pro and con (for and against).

Part 2: Role Play

Form groups of four. Each of you will have a role as Andrew, Betty, Carol, or the **arbiter.** The teacher will give the arbiter one candy bar. The arbiter will listen to arguments from the three teenagers; each will say why he or she wants it and why the others should not get it. The arbiter will award the entire (not divided) candy bar to the teenager who offers the best arguments. (The arbiter will also get a candy bar.)

Writing Assignment

Write your own opinion on *How the Candy Bar Should Be Distributed Justly.* Your written opinion should be at least one-half page and no longer than one page.

You are writing a philosophical argument. To do this, you must not only present your opinion but also show why the alternative solutions are not so good. Here you must pay attention to the principle of *charity*—a philosophical argument that entails considering only the strongest arguments opposite to yours. If you can destroy the strongest opposing arguments, the weaker ones will automatically fall. When dealing with opposing arguments, you will ignore, for example, the argument that "Andrew should get the whole candy bar because his name starts with the letter A." There are stronger arguments for Andrew getting it all.

⫸ iBT Preparation

Independent Speaking Task

Students sit in two rows, facing each other. The teacher will read the task. One row will be the speakers, and the other will be the listeners. The speakers will have 15 to 30 seconds (teacher will decide time allotment) to prepare a response of 45 to 60 seconds. When finished, speakers move to the desk immediately to the left and repeat the exercise with a new partner. When speakers have completed the task twice, they become the listeners, so that each student can speak twice. The second time speakers give their response, there will be no preparation time.

Integrated Speaking Task

Read the following passage, then listen to the passage that the teacher will read. Take notes on both. The teacher will also read a question. You will have 30 seconds to prepare your response. Again, speakers and listeners are in two rows. This time, the speakers respond only once, and then roles are switched.

> *Some Americans believe that Cuba's communist government will fall in the near future and will be replaced by democracy. Hundreds of thousands of Cubans left Cuba and came to the United States after the revolution of 1959. The Castro government seized property that now has a value of more than 50 billion dollars.*

The Race

Objectives

- analytic thinking

- creativity in argument

- to practice using *Conversation Cues* for *Strong Disagreement*

Introduction

In any college course you may take, you will have to establish criteria for your decisions. But are the criteria philosophically rigid or fixed in stone?

Vocabulary Gloss

track	= sport of running various distances, jumping, and so forth
make the team	= meet the criteria for being on the team
tripped	= made someone fall by interfering with leg motion
sluggish	= tired and slow-moving, having no energy
steroid	= substance created in the body that can be manufactured and injected into the body; often done by athletes who want to improve their performance

Part 1

The high school **track** team is going to hold a race. The race will determine who is to **make the team.** Anyone who runs the 100-meter race in 12 seconds or under that is on the team. Jesse, Harry, Carlos, and Ben fail to meet the criterion, but each of them demands a second chance.

Consider the reasons that each of them gives, and decide whether that runner's claim is valid—that is, if he should be given a second chance. Assume that all the stories are true and that there is room for more on the track team.

a. Jesse says that Fred **tripped** him. This is clear from the videotape. It also looks like Fred tripped him deliberately. Should Fred be disqualified?

Jesse says that Fred tripped him.

b. Harry says that the other guys ate his breakfast so that he would not have enough energy to run fast. It is true that the other guys don't like him much and also true that Harry runs better after a good breakfast. He also ran out of vitamins that day, and we know that they always make him run faster.

c. Carlos says he felt very **sluggish** that day and was probably fighting off a cold. His father was a star runner, as was his grandfather. Carlos wants more than anything to make his father proud of him and to follow in his father's footsteps. He says his family would die of disappointment if he didn't make the team.

d. Ben says he had a headache on the day of the race. He has always been in trouble with the law. When he was on the junior high track team last year, he managed to stay out of trouble for the first time in his life. He is afraid that if he doesn't make the team he will start stealing again.

Procedure

1. As a class, briefly discuss each case.

2. Break into small groups, and try to reach a consensus. Everyone must state his or her opinion on each case.

3. Report your group's consensus to the class.

Part 2

You have tried but failed to make the track team. Prepare a reason for getting a second chance. You will be divided into small groups again, with different people, and one student will be appointed as mediator. Only one student in each group will be given a second chance—the one with the most convincing and believable argument. Begin clockwise from the mediator, presenting your reason(s) for a second chance. The other students should criticize these reasons. Feel free to interrupt at any time.

Conversation Cues

Keep your book open to this page or write the cues on a separate piece of paper. Put a check mark next to a cue each time you use it.

Strong Disagreement

> *Are you kidding?*
> *You must be joking!*
> *Come off it!*
> *You can't be serious.*
> *Surely, you jest.*
> *Get real!*
> *No way!*
> *Come on!*

Usage Notes

Surely, you jest is an old, formal, and humorous expression. *Jest* means "joke."

Writing Assignment: Criteria for Accepting Claims for a Second Chance

Which claims, if any, did you accept? Why not accept all the claims? Why accept some and not others? What criteria underlie your choice?

You may write about Jesse, Ben, Carlos, and Harry; or you may write about the group experience in Part 2. Your paper should be about a page.

⫸ iBT Preparation

Independent Speaking Task

Students sit in two rows, facing each other. The teacher will read the task. One row will be the speakers, and the other will be the listeners. The speakers will have 15 to 30 seconds (teacher will decide time allotment) to prepare a response of 45 to 60 seconds. When finished, speakers move to the desk immediately to the left and repeat the exercise with a new partner. When speakers have completed the task twice, they become the listeners, so that each student can speak twice. The second time speakers give their response, there will be no preparation time.

Integrated Speaking Task

Read the following passage, then listen to the passage that the teacher will read. Take notes on both. The teacher will also read a question. You will have 30 seconds to prepare your response. Again, speakers and listeners are in two rows. This time, the speakers respond only once, and then roles are switched.

> *In many sports, athletes have been using steroids or other illegal substances to enhance their performance. This has resulted in many scandals. For instance, Barry Bonds, baseball's homerun king, has been implicated in steroid use. The Tour de France bicycle race is full of such scandals. The 2006 winner, Floyd Landis, was disqualified for use of an illegal anabolic **steroid**.*

The International View

In your country, are criteria for making teams or for getting into schools rigidly applied? Or are they flexible? Do individual circumstances mean a lot in bending criteria? Think of a specific example.

Mrs. Kerr and Ms. Pink

Objectives

- to explore our beliefs about the right of transference of property

- (secondarily) to consider animal rights

Introduction

This scenario is based on an actual event that took place in upper New York State some years ago. The basic principles that you will discuss relate not only to philosophy but to law.

Vocabulary Gloss

widow	= woman whose husband has died
poodle	= pretty little dog with thick, curly hair
show . . . off	= to display with pride
dazzling	= brilliantly shining, very impressive
mink	= animal whose fur is used for very expensive coats
lavish	= spend large sums of money carelessly

Procedure

Read the two parts carefully. In small groups, discuss Ms. Pink's contentions, which appear in Part 1. You will be assigned for homework a role for Part 2. See the Procedure section that follows Part 2 for further instructions.

Part 1

A rich old **widow,** Mrs. Kerr, lives at 300 Central Park West in New York City. She has a **poodle,** which she claims is her only friend in the world. Her greatest (and only) joy in life is taking the poodle for a walk in the park every morning to **show** him **off.** The poodle is a **dazzling** sight and not an uncommon one in New York City. He has a **mink** jacket worth $3,000, a diamond necklace worth $50,000, a jeweled crown worth $20,000, and diamond earrings worth another $20,000.

Ms. Pink, a homeless woman, takes a walk in Central Park every day at the same time Mrs. Kerr does. Ms. Pink says it is unjust that Mrs. Kerr **lavish** all that wealth on an animal. She says (1) that the jewelry should be taken away by the state and given to needy, starving people. She also says (2) that a law should be passed making it illegal to spend more than $1,000 on a pet.

What do you think of Ms. Pink's two contentions?

Ms. Pink says it is unjust that Mrs. Kerr lavish all that wealth on an animal.

<u>Part 2</u>

Mrs. Kerr dies, leaving all her money to her poodle until the animal dies, at which time it will all go to charity. How ironic it is that, after a long search by lawyers, it turns out that Mrs. Kerr's closest relative is . . . Ms. Pink!—her long lost twin sister, separated from her shortly after birth by a shipwreck.

Ms. Pink contests Mrs. Kerr's will in court. It seems that Mrs. Kerr also instructed in her will that her big summerhouse, located on a large estate in the mountains of upstate New York, be burned down with everything in it. She has made a generous gift to the fire department to supervise the burning.

The property on which the estate is located will be donated to charity.

- Is it just that the poodle get the money?
- Is it just that the house be burned down?

Procedure for Role Play

Half of class will be instructed to prepare for the role of Mrs. Kerr, and the other half, Ms. Pink. Mrs. Kerr is on her deathbed and has just written her will, assigning all of her property to her poodle. Ms. Pink has just been made aware that she is the only living relative of Mrs. Kerr. You must invent all the details of your lives: where you have lived, your life history, how you were separated, and so forth. Practice speaking to yourself, reviewing all the facets of your (new) life.

In class you will be divided into groups of three: Mrs. Kerr, Ms. Pink, and an arbiter. The arbiter judges the case objectively (forgetting the life history that he or she has prepared for Mrs. Kerr or Ms. Pink), based entirely on the arguments given by the players. When all the groups are finished, each arbiter will tell the class why he or she chose to validate or invalidate the will.

⫸ iBT Preparation

Independent Speaking Task

Students sit in two rows, facing each other. The teacher will read the task. One row will be the speakers, and the other will be the listeners. The speakers will have 15 to 30 seconds (teacher will decide time allotment) to prepare a response of 45 to 60 seconds. When finished, speakers move to the desk immediately to the left and repeat the exercise with a new partner. When speakers have completed the task twice, they become the listeners, so that each student can speak twice. The second time speakers give their response, there will be no preparation time.

Integrated Speaking Task

Read the following passage, then listen to the passage that the teacher will read. Take notes on both. The teacher will also read a question. You will have 30 seconds to prepare your response. Again, speakers and listeners are in two rows. This time, the speakers respond only once, and then roles are switched.

> *In the United States, dogfighting is illegal in all but two states. Still, it is a multibillion dollar industry, and around 30,000 people participate in the illegal activity where two dogs, usually pit bulls, fight each other, often resulting in the death of one of the dogs. The activity, which some people call a sport, has been denounced as cruel and barbaric.*

Finders, Keepers

Objective

- to reflect on the basic philosophical issue of property rights and to articulate your thoughts

Introduction

In any introductory philosophy course, you will face the issue of property rights. This exercise will help you feel comfortable dealing with the issue. You will understand what the problems are, and you will be able to articulate your own view. Your views will be changed and enriched by hearing the ideas of your classmates. At the same time, you will have fun in the discussion.

Along the way, you will deal with philosopher John Locke's famous **proviso** that you can do what you want with property as long as there is "enough and as good left in common for others."

You should be stimulated to think about how anyone happens to own anything.

Introductory Question

For homework and in preparation for class, think about this: Do parents own their children? The next class will start with a brief debate on this topic. Read the Finders, Keepers scenario for homework, to prepare to discuss this question in small groups: Is it just that Stuart retain sole possession of all the goods?

Also, for homework, think of five items that you would add to the list of items found by Stuart.

Procedure

Your small group is the class that has been shipwrecked. Decide how the goods are to be distributed. One of you will volunteer for or will be assigned the role of Stuart. When you have finished, each group will tell the class what distribution it actually made and how the distribution was decided on.

Vocabulary Gloss

proviso	= a condition in a contract
shipwrecked	= having one's ship sunk
on the spur of the moment	= deciding instantly
can't help but X	= can't avoid doing X
scout	= look around
mourn	= feel sad at the death or loss of

You, the students of this class, have been **shipwrecked.** Fortunately, you all survived, swimming to the shores of the uninhabited tropical island of Nadur with just the shirts on your backs. Unfortunately, no one knows where you are. No one even knows that you all had left, **on the spur of the moment,** for a cruise on one student's boat.

Although you'd rather be home again, you **can't help but** find the island a paradise. The climate is delightfully warm, day and night. There are no dangerous animals to contend with. Fruit of all kinds grows plentifully on trees. Vegetables grow wild.

You miss, however, your iPods and all the comforts of home. All of your belongings went down with the ship. Now, on the morning after the shipwreck, you gather together on the beach and decide to **scout** about the small island. Only one of your classmates is missing—Stuart. You **mourn** him, but not too much—nobody cared a great deal for him anyway. But as it turns out, Stuart is not dead—he is just an early riser, and he has already gone off to scout the island. When you encounter the big, strong Stuart an hour later, he is standing proudly on a group of boxes he has retrieved, with his own labor, from the edge of the sea. He has just concluded an inventory. These boxes, which are not from your ship, contain the following items.

3 bottles of Dom Perignon champagne

1 volleyball net and ball

2 mosquito nets

3 fishing poles

1 bottle of quinine

1 standard first aid kit

1 gun with ammunition

3 plastic containers of sunscreen

1 thousand-dollar bill

Write in five more items your group agrees on.

_____

_____

_____

_____

_____

You approach Stuart with broad smiles that turn to frowns as Stuart says, "Finders, keepers!"

A careful search of the island turns up nothing more. But, in fact, at present you do not need any of the items Stuart has assembled.

⫸ iBT Preparation

Independent Speaking Task

Students sit in two rows, facing each other. The teacher will read the task. One row will be the speakers, and the other will be the listeners. The speakers will have 15 to 30 seconds (teacher will decide time allotment) to prepare a response of 45 to 60 seconds. When finished, speakers move to the desk immediately to the left and repeat the exercise with a new partner. When speakers have completed the task twice, they become the listeners, so that each student can speak twice. The second time speakers give their response, there will be no preparation time.

Integrated Speaking Task

Read the following passage, then listen to the passage that the teacher will read. Take notes on both. The teacher will also read a question. You will have 30 seconds to prepare your response. Again, speakers and listeners are in two rows. This time, the speakers respond only once, then roles are switched.

> *Some philosophers and economists find taxation immoral. They think that taxation is really forced labor—slavery. If you tax me, you are forcing me to work for you, and that is unjust and immoral. Others argue that nobody should be allowed to starve in the street or have no health care, and taxation is the best way to provide for this social minimum.*

The International View

Does your country have a strong tradition of private property? Are there things that cannot be owned privately but must belong to all the people?

Joe, His Bread, and the Lifeboat

Objectives

- to examine how deeply we believe in property rights

- to develop criteria for a just distribution of goods

Introduction

Lifeboat scenarios are often used to push our beliefs to an extreme. When you make your own arguments, in any subject, you may want to use a similar scenario to test some principle. For a principle or a belief to be valid, it must apply in all cases. Therefore, you create an extreme situation. If the principle is valid here, it should be valid in all cases. The scenario that we discuss here may have a happy ending.

> ## Vocabulary Gloss
>
> **drifting** = moving on a current of water, without power
>
> **rowing** = using oars to move a boat

Procedure

In small groups, answer the questions that are part of this scenario.

Ten men are in a lifeboat at sea. They have been **drifting** for five days and have consumed, they think, all of their food. Everyone is very hungry, because they have been **rowing** for five days in hope of reaching land. At first they had a reasonable expectation of success. Now, however, only Arnold has strength enough to row.

Suddenly, Joe reaches into his bag and finds a loaf of bread that his wife had baked to help him in case of just such an emergency. He smiles and thanks his wife for her wise and lifesaving thought.

1. Does Joe have a right to eat all the bread by himself, as he would like to do?
2. Should he share it with all the others equally?
3. Some of the men are much bigger than the others and need more to survive. Should they get more?
4. Arnold thinks he should get it all. Does he have a good case for his suggestion?
5. Since Arnold is the only one still strong enough to row, he is also capable of taking the bread from Joe by force and eating it all. If the other men don't agree with Arnold's suggestion, does he have a right to take it?

The International View

Is there ever starvation in your country, or are the hungry always taken care of by the government or by family or relatives?

Sam and the Posse

Objective

- to test our beliefs about property rights

Introduction

Most of us believe that what is ours is ours—in other words, that we have rights over our property. If I leave my hat in your car, it does not become yours, right? I can demand that you give it back, right? We will test these assumptions. (This scenario is similar to one devised by philosopher Immanuel Kant and may prepare you for discussion aspects of Kant's philosophy, as well as property rights.)

Procedure

In small groups, discuss the questions that follow the scenario about Sam. When you finish, the teacher will elicit a quick summary of responses to the situation.

Vocabulary Gloss

slain	= (past participle of *slay*) killed
in cold blood	= mercilessly, with no remorse
ammunition	= bullets (what is put in a gun)
homicidal	= having tendency to kill
posse	= group of community members loosely organized by local law enforcement officials to hunt down a criminal
banning	= officially prohibiting

Sam is a killer and is being hunted by the sons of the man he has just **slain in cold blood.** He has a gun but no **ammunition.** He comes to your house and demands the box of ammunition he left there last week. Of course, you didn't know at that time what a **homicidal** maniac he was. The sounds of the **posse** can be heard outside. Sam is sure that they will shoot him dead. Will you give him his box of ammunition? Exactly what will you do? What does your decision say about your view of property rights?

⏵ iBT Preparation

Independent Speaking Task

Students sit in two rows, facing each other. The teacher will read the task. One row will be the speakers, and the other will be the listeners. The speakers will have 15 to 30 seconds (teacher will decide time allotment) to prepare a response of 45 to 60 seconds. When finished, speakers move to the desk immediately to the left and repeat the exercise with a new partner. When speakers have completed the task twice, they become the listeners, so that each student can speak twice. The second time speakers give their response, there will be no preparation time.

Integrated Speaking Task

Read the following passage, then listen to the passage that the teacher will read. Take notes on both. The teacher will also read a question. You will have 30 seconds to prepare your response. Again, speakers and listeners are in two rows. This time, the speakers respond only once, then roles are switched.

> *Many Americans believe that citizens have a right to possess a gun. When people advocate the **banning** of handguns or automatic rifles, they say: "Guns don't kill people. People do." Others say that if that is true, then it's okay for people to have atomic bombs because bombs don't kill people; people do.*

The International View

Who has the right to own a gun in your country? Everyone? In your opinion, should this right be extended to more people or restricted to fewer?

3

Law

Crime and Punishment

Objectives

- to understand the U.S. judicial system and how it differs from others

- to understand the complexity and difficulty of applying concepts to real events

Introduction

In any course you take, you will have to define terms, and the definition must work in real situations. In this unit we will see that "murder" depends on the concept of "intention." But though we use this word with no problem, it is not as simple as it appears.

Before going any further, we need to understand more fully the U.S. judicial system. The system is called *common law* and is similar to England's system. It differs in some respects from European and other judicial systems. Whenever you notice a difference, mention it. The comparison will be interesting and useful.

In American law, we draw an objective line between *wrongdoing* (the crime) and *attribution* (excuses based on particular circumstances). If you are insane, the wrongdoing cannot be attributed to you. If you are pregnant and starving when you steal, you are less guilty.

In European law, attribution tends to be built into the crime. So, whereas in the United States a crime might be called *homicide* (killing), in Europe there would be more specific categories for the crime like *homicide by insanity*.

In criminal justice, problems arise because language is often ambiguous. For example, the crime of murder depends on the notion of *intention*. In order for a crime to be classified as a murder, there must be *clear intention*. But without a confession, we can only guess at a person's intention. This raises serious problems. Think about the following questions and scenarios, and then write your opinions underneath the scenarios (unless your teacher asks you to write them on a separate sheet of paper and hand them in). Be prepared to discuss your opinions in class.

Scenarios 4 and 8 are similar to events in the films *Mortal Thoughts* and *Reversal of Fortune*. These films raise interesting questions about the problematic nature of *intention*, which is necessary for a crime to be murder. The class may want to see these films.

Vocabulary Gloss

diabetic	= person having disease of diabetes (high blood sugar)
insulin	= medication taken by diabetics
cyanide	= poison
syringe	= hypodermic needle
shot	= injection
tumor	= an abnormal mass of tissue growth
crib	= baby's enclosed bed
bum	= lazy, unsuccessful person who doesn't work
arsenic	= poison
go off	= explode
remorse	= sorrow or guilt over past wrongdoing
dismantles	= takes apart
hijacked	= forcibly took control of vehicle
rapist	= person who rapes (forces sexual intercourse)

suffocates	=	dies from lack of air
at the end of her rope	=	psychologically unable to continue in the situation
coroner	=	doctor who determines cause of death
appendicitis	=	inflammation of the appendix, an organ in the lower-right side of the abdomen
surgeon	=	doctor who operates
delirious	=	mentally disturbed, extremely confused
strangles	=	kills by squeezing throat and stopping breathing
torture	=	physical abuse that causes great physical or emotional pain
deprivation	=	being without something, being denied something

Procedure

Read each scenario at home, and decide on your responses. Discuss them as a class, in small groups, or both. In all cases, one student reads the scenario, and the teacher calls on students to give their opinions, which will be either read or spoken (preferably the latter). Ask questions about the vocabulary after the reading. Try to reach a consensus. When you have finished, the teacher will ask each group to tell the class its consensus opinion of all or of selected scenarios.

If you recall any similar scenarios, make sure to share them with the class.

1. George plans to kill his wife, who is a **diabetic.** He plans to inject her with poison. Alan learns of this and substitutes **insulin** in the bottle of **cyanide.** George fills up the **syringe** and gives her a good-bye **shot.** She survives. Then Alan tells the police.

    Is George guilty of a crime? If so, what is it? What could George say in his defense? What role does *intention* play here?

2. A man goes to the top of a ten-story tower in Texas with a rifle and starts firing at a crowd of people from a distance of about 100 meters. Two people die. Is this murder?

3. A man with a brain **tumor** opens a window on the third floor of his house, walks to his son's **crib,** picks him up, and throws him out the window. Everyone says that he loved his son. Is this murder?

4. Roseann plans to kill her husband, an unfaithful **bum.** She mixes enough **arsenic** to kill an elephant into some sugar and asks her daughter to carry the sugar bowl upstairs to the bum, who is screaming for his sugar. She trips on the stairs, and Fido, their dog, licks the "sugar" and falls over dead. The clever daughter sweeps up the mess, throws it away along with Fido, puts real sugar in the bowl, and delivers it to her dad. Has Roseann committed a crime? Did she have the *intention* to kill?

5. Ed, a terrorist, plants a time bomb in the Park Street station, set to **go off** at rush hour. He goes home, turns on the news, and is suddenly struck with **remorse.** He rushes back to the station to turn off the bomb but arrives a half hour late. Fortunately, the bomb was defective and did not go off. He takes it back home and **dismantles** it. Has Ed committed a crime? How does *intention* figure into it?

6. Ed's twin sister Edwina is a stewardess on an airplane that has been **hijacked** by the terrible and infamous terrorist Patty Hearts. She orders the captain to change course and fly over Cuba. Expecting that Patty might use a parachute, Edwina cuts it with a knife. The terrorist has not harmed anyone. Patty jumps out with the defective chute and dies. Is Edwina guilty of murder? Of anything?

7. A **rapist** places his hand over his victim's mouth, simply to keep her from calling for help. She **suffocates** and dies. Is this murder?

8. Roseann is **at the end of her rope.** She can't take another minute of living with Hannibal. While he is sleeping, she stabs him through the heart with a steak knife. She leans over to kiss him good-bye and notices that his forehead is cold. The **coroner** reports that Hannibal died of a drug overdose four hours earlier. Is Roseann guilty of a crime?

Roseann can't stand another minute of living with Hannibal.

9. Jules and Jim are in love with the same woman. Independently, they decide that Paris (the city where they live) is not big enough for both of them. Then, suddenly, Jim has an attack of **appendicitis**. Unfortunately for him, Jules is a skilled **surgeon.** He plans to make a regrettable mistake at the local hospital. Jim, almost **delirious** with pain, looks up from the surgery table at Jules' smiling face. He grabs Jules by the throat and **strangles** him to death. Who is guilty of what?

⫸ iBT Preparation

Independent Speaking Task

Students sit in two rows, facing each other. The teacher will read the task. One row will be the speakers, and the other will be the listeners. The speakers will have 15 to 30 seconds (teacher will decide time allotment) to prepare a response of 45 to 60 seconds. When finished, speakers move to the desk immediately to the left and repeat the exercise with a new partner. When speakers have completed the task twice, they become the listeners, so that each student can speak twice. The second time speakers give their response, there will be no preparation time.

<u>**Integrated Speaking Task**</u>

Read the following passage, then listen to the passage that the teacher will read. Take notes on both. The teacher will also read a question. You will have 30 seconds to prepare your response. Again, speakers and listeners are in two rows. This time, the speakers respond only once, then roles are switched.

> *Since the United States was attacked on September 11, 2001, there has been considerable debate about whether **torture** should be allowed in some circumstances. A 2006 BBC poll found that 59 percent of people worldwide rejected torture. A poll in the United States found that most Americans rejected leaving prisoners naked and chained in uncomfortable positions for hours. But the poll found that a majority of Americans thought that sleep **deprivation** was not torture.*

The International View

In your legal system, is the accused assumed to be innocent until proven guilty or assumed guilty until proven innocent? Which of these legal assumptions do you think is better?

Is there capital punishment (the death penalty) for murder in your country?

Presentation

Choose two students to present their views on capital punishment (one for and one against). Each will have a predetermined amount of time (e.g., three minutes) to present his or her point of view. Do not read your views, but you may use note cards to help you remember what you want to say. When the presentation is done, the rest of the class may offer their views.

Humor in the Court

Objective

- to understand and appreciate humor in English

Introduction

The dialogues that follow are real, not fictional. As you will see, humor can arise in the most serious situations. Although law is a very serious matter and profession, it involves ordinary people, and not all lawyers and prosecutors are brilliant. (The dialogues are from *More Humor in the Court* by Mary Louise Gilman [Vienna, VA: National Court Reporters' Association, 1984].)

Vocabulary Gloss

lumbar region	= lower back
deceased	= dead
pursuant to	= following
scalp	= skin on top of head
skin graft	= attachment of skin from one part of the body to another part or from one person to another
buttocks	= part of body that you sit on
fracas	= a noisy quarrel

Procedure

As you read these dialogues, note the one or ones that you find most funny. In class, read one and tell why it is funny. Also, note any examples that you don't understand. In class, your fellow students will explain them.

1. *Q:* What is your brother-in-law's name?

   A: Borofkin.

   Q: What's his first name?

   A: I can't remember.

   Q: He's been your brother-in-law for years, and you can't remember his first name?

   A: No. I tell you I'm too excited. (Rising from the witness chair and pointing to Mr. Borofkin.) Nathan, for God's sake, tell them your first name!

2. *Q:* Did you ever stay all night with this man in New York?

   A: I refuse to answer that question.

   Q: Did you ever stay all night with this man in Chicago?

   A: I refuse to answer that question.

   Q: Did you ever stay all night with this man in Miami?

   A: No.

3. *Q:* Now, Mrs. Johnson, how was your first marriage terminated?

   A: By death.

   Q: And by whose death was it terminated?

4. *Q:* Doctor, did you say he was shot in the woods?

   A: No, I said he was shot in the **lumbar region.**

5. *Q:* What is your name?

   A: Ernestine McDowell.

   Q: And what is your marital status?

   A: Fair.

6. *Q:* Are you married?

   A: No, I'm divorced.

   Q: And what did your husband do before you divorced him?

   A: A lot of things I didn't know about.

7. *Q:* Do you know how far pregnant you are right now?

   A: I will be three months November 8th.

   Q: Apparently, then, the date of conception was August 8th?

   A: Yes.

   Q: What were you and your husband doing at that time?

8. *Q:* Mrs. Smith, do you believe that you are emotionally unstable?

   A: I should be.

   Q: How many times have you committed suicide?

   A: Four times.

9. *Q:* Doctor, how many autopsies have you performed on dead people?

   A: All my autopsies have been performed on dead people.

10. *Q:* Were you acquainted with the **deceased?**

    A: Yes, sir.

    Q: Before or after he died?

11. *Q:* Officer, what led you to believe the defendant was under the influence [of alcohol]?

    A: Because he was "argumentary" and he couldn't "pronunciate" his words.

12. *Q:* What happened then?

    A: He told me, he says, "I have to kill you because you can identify me."

    Q: Did he kill you?

    A: No.

13. *Q:* Mrs. Jones, is your appearance this morning **pursuant to** a deposition notice which I sent to your attorney?

    A: No. This is how I dress when I go to work.

14. *Q:* Did he pick the dog up by the ears?

    A: No.

    Q: What was he doing with the dog's ears?

    A: Picking them up in the air.

    Q: Where was the dog at this time?

    A: Attached to the ears.

15. *Q:* And lastly, Gary, all your responses must be oral. Okay? What school do you go to?

    A: Oral.

    Q: How old are you?

    A: Oral.

16. *Q:* What is your relationship with the plaintiff?

    A: She is my daughter.

    Q: Was she your daughter on February 13, 1979?

17. *Q:* Now, you have investigated other murders, have you not, where there was a victim?

18. *Q:* Did you tell your lawyer that your husband had offered you indignities?

    A: He didn't offer me nothing; he just said I could have the furniture.

19. *Q:* So, after the anesthesia, when you came out of it, what did you observe with respect to your **scalp?**

    A: I didn't see my scalp the whole time I was in the hospital.

    Q: It was covered?

    A: Yes, bandaged.

    Q: Then, later on . . . what did you see?

    A: I had a **skin graft.** My whole **buttocks** and leg were removed and put on top of my head.

20. *Q:* Could you see him from where you were standing?

    A: I could see his head.

    Q: And where was his head?

    A: Just above his shoulders.

21. *Q:* Are you qualified to give a urine sample?

    A: Yes, I have been since early childhood.

22. *Q:* The truth of the matter is that you were not an unbiased, objective witness, isn't it? You too were shot in the **fracas?**

    A: No, sir. I was shot midway between the fracas and the navel.

23. *Q:* (showing man picture) That's you?

    A: Yes, sir.

    Q: And you were present when the picture was taken, right?

24. *Q:* Was that the same nose you broke as a child?

The International View

Can you recall any strange or funny court stories from your country?

Organ Transplantation

Objectives

- to be conversant on a topic that has two compelling philosophical and legal sides

- to form a better opinion on an issue that directly concerns you

Introduction

In your lifetime you may need an organ transplant or you may be asked by a family member to give one, since organs donated by family members tend to be rejected by the recipient's body less frequently. These are difficult choices, and they raise issues that don't always have clear answers. You will profit from hearing other students' opinions on these issues and clarifying your own. Students may want to rent a DVD of the movie "Dirty Pretty Things," (2003) directed by Stephen Frears, about an illegal Nigerian immigrant in London who had been a doctor in his own country and is coerced into operating on patients who are selling a kidney. It has a happy ending.

Removing a section of the liver has a risk factor of less than one percent. For kidney donation, the risk of death is .03 percent, almost negligible, according to the *New England Journal of Medicine.* But around 6,000 people will die in one year waiting for kidneys or livers. *(These statistics from: www.capmag.com/article.asp?ID=4326.)*

Vocabulary Gloss

cardiac arrest = heart attack

corneas = membranes that cover the pupil and iris of the eye

oncologist = doctor specializing in cancer treatment

pancreas = organ near the stomach that secretes juices into intestine

kidney = an organ that filters waste material from the blood

liver	= large reddish-brown organ in upper abdomen that removes waste from the blood
marrow	= soft tissue that fills central cavities of bones
foster	= encourage the development of something

Procedure

Read the following and answer the questions, and then discuss each question in groups, coming up with a consensus answer.

The Solvable Problem of Organ Shortages

by Jane E. Brody
New York Times, August 28, 2007

The number of donor organs falls far short of the need. As of June (2007), 97,000 people awaited lifesaving transplants, and each day the waiting list grows five times faster than the donation rate.

People typically wait three to five years for donated organs, and each day 17 of them die. But, as Dr. Moritsugo (acting surgeon general of the United States) noted recently in the Journal of the American Dietetic Association, "The shortage of donor organs is a medical problem for which there is a cure." When the decision is made to donate, he said, those families, "often in a time of grief and tragedy, rise above personal concern to help others in need of lifesaving transplantation."

The parents of Laurie McLendon, 42, chose to donate when their daughter suffered **cardiac arrest**. Two women received her kidneys, a burn unit received skin, her **corneas** went to an eye bank, and her liver was transplanted into a 61-year-old pediatric **oncologist**.

Other organs and tissues that can be donated are the heart, **pancreas,** lungs, intestines, bone marrow, heart valves and connective tissue. A **kidney,** part of a **liver,** lobe of a lung, and bone **marrow** can be obtained from living donors. But three out of four transplanted organs come from people who die and had indicated their willingness to be donors by signing an advance directive or by telling the person designated to speak for them when they can no longer speak for themselves.

There are several ways to increase the supply of organs. They include persuading more people to agree to be donors when they die, putting hospital policies and procedures in place to **foster** organ donation, obtaining more organs donated from the victims of brain death and cardiac death, and increasing the number of live donors, especially people unrelated to the recipients.

Organ Prices

Here is a list of prices on the black market for organs from different countries, found on the *Wired* Internet site. Delivery takes weeks instead of years, and while the price of some organs may seem high, it is often less than the price of transplantation in the United States.

Kidney	Lung
$15,000–40,000 **Pakistan**	$150,000–170,000 **China**
$20,000 **Iraq**	$290,000 **Singapore**
$25,000 **Russia**	$290,000 **South Africa**
$35,000–85,000 **Philippines**	$290,000 **South Korea**
$65,000 **China**	$290,000 **Taiwan**
$80,000 **Colombia**	
$120,000 **South Africa**	
$145,000 **Turkey**	

Liver	Pancreas	Heart
$25,000 **Egypt**	$110,000 **China**	$90,000 **Colombia**
$25,000 **Pakistan**	$140,000 **Singapore**	$130,000–160,000 **China**
$60,000–130,000 **China**	$140,000 **South Africa**	$290,000 **South Africa**
$100,000 **Colombia**	$140,000 **South Korea**	$290,000 **South Korea**
$100,000 **Philippines**	$140,000 **Taiwan**	$290,000 **Taiwan**
$290,000 **Singapore**		$290,000 **Singapore**
$290,000 **South Africa**		
$290,000 **South Korea**		
$290,000 **Taiwan**		

Ads for Organs

Ads selling organs can be found on the Internet, for example
http://xo.typepad .com/blog/2003/11/woman_wanted_to.html#comment-408993.

(Spelling mistakes not corrected.)

I'll sell my kidney for $6000 or best offer that's reasonable.. 33 male very health, America.

I am very poor and I have to pay back a huge amount (debt) Therefore I have decided to sell my kidney, I am healthy 22 years male from Pakistan I will sell kidney just for US$5000.

im looking to sell my kidney to help me live more comfortable whilst im in uni. No less than £10,000, or nearst offer!!?Very serious for the write offer.?respon a.s.a.p

I would glady donate a kidney in return for financial help in getting me out of debt.

I would like to sell my kidney. I am divorced mother of two. I am O neg and am very healthy. I don't drink or smoke and take good care of myself. I do need $10K to make a difference so please respond if you're interested.

i am a 30 yr old male willing to sacrifice a kidney, my blood type is O, i do not drink, and have a very healthy lifestyle. Need help paying for my wifes medical expenses. Help me, and i will help you.

My brothers and I would like to sell one of our Kidney's. There are 3 of us, all are in good shape. Would like $10,000 per Kidney.

I would like to sell mi kidney, because I try to kill me three times and I have a lot of creditors in mi door. Please help me and I help you. My creditors are aroun 20K. If it is too much, you can call me o write me as soon as possible in my email.

Discussion Questions

1. Look at the list of prices for different organs available on the black market in various countries. The donor is paid, probably, about 10 percent of those prices, and sometimes the promised money is never paid. Should the selling of organs be legalized and controlled by the government?

   a. Yes

   b. No

2. We can sell our hair and our blood, so it should be legal to sell our organs.

   a. I agree

   b. I disagree

3. You have two kidneys. You only need one to survive. How much would you sell a kidney for?

   a. $500,000

   b. $1,000,000

   c. no amount. (I would not sell.)

4. If you thought you would probably die of kidney failure and were very low on the list for transplant, would you buy a kidney on the black market?

   a. Yes

   b. No

5. Would you consent to donate your organs for transplantation to save someone's life? Why or why not?

   a. I would

   b. I would not

6. Would you donate your whole body for medical research or education?

   a. Yes

   b. No

   c. Not sure

7. Which is better policy, the American law where you must sign a form to have your organs donated or the European law where you are automatically considered a donor unless you expressly declare that you do not want to be one?

   a. The American law

   b. The European law

8. Even the European law is loose, allowing people to refuse to give their organs for donation. If we can force men into military service, where they might be killed, we should mandate removal of organs from all dead people.

   a. I agree

   b. I disagree

9. We should have a law requiring the payment of a certain sum of money to all citizens who agree to donate their organs after death.

   a. Yes. And the sum should be $_____

   b. No

10. Young people who sign a form to donate their organs after death should have top priority if they need an organ transplant when they are older.

    a. I agree

    b. I disagree

11. If a person seems crazy, suffering psychological disorder or low self-esteem, should the person be allowed to donate a kidney for free while alive, since it seems the motives are compassionate?

    a. Yes

    b. No

12. If a person is revered or is especially needed by society and needs an organ transplant, should that person be moved to the top of the list so that he/she gets the needed organ right away? Consider a beloved ex-president of your country, a living president, or a great soccer player.

    a. Yes

    b. No

13. Look again at the ads for selling kidneys. Do you think it is right for a person, in some circumstances, to sell a kidney? In Iran, organ selling is legal, but when thinking about vending, the majority of a large group of organ sellers had negative feelings or were depressed or felt shunned by society. Eighty-five percent of them responded that, if they had the choice all over again, they would definitely not sell their organs. Under what circumstances, if any, do you think a person should be allowed to see his/her organs? Write your answer here, and then share your answer with your group or with the class.

    _____

    _____

    _____

⫸ iBT Preparation

Independent Speaking Task

Students sit in two rows, facing each other. One row (speakers) will answer the question that the teacher reads. The other row (scorers) will listen to the speech and give it a rating of 1–4, 4 being the highest. Speakers will have 15 to 30 seconds (teacher will decide time allotment) to prepare a response of 45 to 60 seconds. When the conversation between speakers and scorers is finished, the speakers move to the chair to their left and repeat the exercise with a new partner. This time there is no preparation time—candidates already know what they are going to say. After the procedure is repeated twice, scorers become speakers and vice versa.

Integrated Speaking Task

Read the following passage, and then listen to the passage that the teacher will read. Take notes on both. The teacher will also read a question. You will have 30 seconds to prepare your response. Again, speakers and listeners are in two rows. This time, the speakers respond only once, and then roles are switched.

> *Mickey Mantle was a famous baseball player, one of the greatest who ever lived. He played centerfield for the New York Yankees. In 1994, his liver started to fail. He needed a liver transplant soon or he would die. Two days after his name went on the list of those needing liver transplants, his name went to the top of the list.*

4

Ethics

Coercion/Paternalism

Objectives

- to understand the libertarian philosophy of John Stuart Mill

- to understand that while we all want to believe in the concept of "individual liberty" to a strong degree, we sometimes actually place severe restrictions on this concept

- to show that philosophical issues pertain to our everyday lives

- to see how abstract concepts are tested on the hard edge of reality

- to learn to guess the meanings of unknown words

Introduction

Coercion is "forcing someone to do something against his or her will." Coercion may be for a good purpose or a bad purpose, and coercion may be legal or illegal. For instance, a parent may coerce his or her child to eat her spinach, which we assume is a good purpose. A father may coerce a sickly boy to play football in spite of the child's inability to do well and his constant injuries, which we assume is bad.

We also encounter the interesting question of whether or not coercion can lead to good behavior. Some think that a person cannot be coerced into goodness. But a child might pick up his or her daddy's gun and say, "If you two don't stop fighting, I'm going to blow my brains out." And a parent might say to a child, "Be nice to your baby brother or I'll hit you."

Even when used for a bad purpose, coercion may be legal. A parent can be a perfectly cruel **tyrant** (just for the pleasure of dominating the children) and get away with it. Or coercion can be for a good purpose but illegal. (Feel free to disagree with this.) For example, during a **famine,** a rich man might buy all the bread. Someone then might order the rich man, at gunpoint, to give away all the bread. This is coercion—illegal but for a good purpose.

At any rate, coercion is a fascinating and troublesome issue. And one of the most difficult issues related to coercion is *paternalism*. This is the name given to the "state's deciding for the citizens what is good for the citizens." This obviously **infringes on** individual liberty. To the extent that we believe in that liberty, we will disapprove of paternalism. But, in fact, most of us believe in some degree of paternalism, as we shall see.

But let's give *individual liberty* its fair say. The most well-known spokesman for this doctrine is John Stuart Mill, who wrote about the subject in a book entitled *On Liberty* in 1859. Mill was concerned about the tyranny of the majority. Any time people join together to form a state, they give up some of their rights to the state. Drawing the line between individual and state rights is a difficult task, but it is important because the state is much more powerful than the individual and it can abuse its power.

Mill puts the case for individual liberty very strongly.

> . . . the sole end for which mankind are warranted, individually or collectively, in interfering with the liberty of action of any of their number is self-protection. That the only purpose for which power can be rightfully exercised over any member of a civilized community, against his own will, is to prevent harm to others. His own good, either physical or moral, is not a sufficient **warrant.** (boldface added)

Mill contends that a person cannot be coerced to do something because it will make him or her happier, wiser, or better or even because it is the right thing to do. You can argue with and reason with the person, but you cannot coerce him or her. "Over himself, over his own body and mind, the individual is **sovereign,**" says Mill.

Do you believe Mill's thesis? Keep his arguments in mind as we investigate specific cases of paternalism. If you believe in Mill 100 percent, you can call yourself a *libertarian*.

Vocabulary Gloss

tyrant	= ruler with complete power, brutal and oppressive
famine	= widespread lack of food/starvation
infringes on	= interferes with a right or privilege
warrant	= permit
sovereign	= self-governing
lucidly	= clearly
bungee jumping	= jumping from great height with elastic (bungee) cords attached to one's ankles

Vocabulary Learning Technique

Throughout this book you will find Vocabulary Gloss sections in which the most difficult words will be defined for you. These will enable you to prepare your homework efficiently. However, there will always be other words in the readings that you do not know. When this occurs, instead of looking up every word in the dictionary, you should try to guess the meanings of the words from the context. You will often find that you can guess with a strong degree of confidence. Of course, you can never be totally sure that you are correct, but proceeding with a certain level of confidence—which you must determine for yourself—will allow you to work much faster.

For example, let's assume you do not know the word *humongous*.

Suppose that you encounter the sentence, "My SUV is such a *humongous* car it doesn't fit in my garage." What meaning would you guess for this word?

If you guessed "very big" you would be correct.

Now let's look at a word that appears in the context of this chapter. In the Procedure section that follows, you will read this scenario: "Suppose a man decides to jump out of a window believing that he will float upward. You reason with him unsuccessfully. Will you *restrain* him physically?"

Perhaps you do not understand the word *restrain*. Could you guess its meaning? What words could we substitute for *restrain* that would make sense? *Push? Shoot? Talk? Stop? Prevent? Hold?*

If you thought any of the last three, *stop, prevent,* or *hold,* you would be correct enough. You would not need to look up the word.

Once you learn to trust your own reasonable guesses from context, your reading will go much faster.

Procedure

Read the scenarios, think about the cases, and then write your opinion in the space provided. In class, one student will read each scenario, and you will be asked to read or speak your opinion. You will be expected to defend your position with logical arguments.

1. Suppose a man decides to jump out of a window believing that he will float upward. You reason with him unsuccessfully. Will you restrain him physically? If so, you are acting paternalistically.

   Write your answer here.

   _____

   _____

Introduction to Question 2

Gerald Dworkin, a philosopher, thinks paternalism is justified in some cases—when it preserves for the individual his ability to carry out his own decisions rationally in the future.

2. Suppose you encounter an old man who is in constant pain both from cancer and from a half dozen diseases connected with old age. He tells you very **lucidly** that he wishes to commit suicide by swallowing an overdose of sleeping pills. If you stop him, you will preserve his ability to make rational choices in the future. Will you stop him?

   Write your answer here.

   _____

   _____

Introduction to Questions 3–5

Norman Daniels, another philosopher, thinks that paternalism is justified in cases where (1) *competency* for rational action is missing or (2) *voluntariness* is missing. In other words, if the state decides you are not acting rationally, it can restrain you. And if the state feels that you are somehow being coerced to do something, it can restrict your liberty to do it.

Others think that the state should act to prevent people from endangering themselves. But then the state would have to ban any number of activities. *Should the state ban the following?* Add to the list any topic you think would fit and ask the group for their opinions on it.

Should the state ban bungee jumping?

3. **Bungee jumping**

Write your answer here.

_____

_____

4. Boxing

Write your answer here.

_____

_____

5. Eating blowfish (fugu) in Japan. Read the text on pages 59–61, and study the vocabulary that precedes it.

Write your answer here.

_____

_____

Vocabulary Gloss

innocuous	= not likely to offend or harm
penchant	= tendency
knocked off	= killed
stabbed	= deliberately injured with a knife
dabbed	= put one object lightly in contact with another (usually liquid or powder)
secretions	= products (usually liquid) released by the body of an organism
flops	= swings, bounces, or falls clumsily
goner	= person or animal soon to die
numbness	= inability to feel; insensitivity to pain or pleasure
lethal	= deadly
Russian roulette	= dangerous game of putting one bullet in a gun and firing at your head with 1/6 chance of killing yourself
toxic	= poisonous
relented	= became less severe
sliver	= small, thin piece
set . . . back	= cost (verb)
gourmand	= person who loves good food
hauled	= pulled, carried
plump	= slightly fat
fare	= something to eat
wriggling	= moving like a snake
banned	= prohibited
realm	= kingdom; area under king's control
white-collar	= relating to jobs that receive salaries

Why Japanese gourmands will die for a taste of fugu

By Colin Nickerson
GLOBE STAFF

Shimonoseki, Japan–Rank has its privileges, but the emperor and empress of Japan are denied one privilege that many Japanese consider a gastronomic birthright: the eating of fugu.

Fuss and fume though their highnesses may, the haughty chamberlains responsible for running the royal household decreed years ago that the **innocuous**-looking fugu—also known as globefish—is fare unfit for the imperial palate.

It is not a matter of taste, but of poison.

The intestines, liver and sexual organs of the fugu, a Japanese delicacy, contain tetrodotoxin, a paralyzing substance reckoned to be 500 times more deadly than cyanide.

The Japanese taste for raw seafood is well known; their **penchant** for fugu is incomprehensible.

This is the fish, after all, that nearly **knocked off** James Bond. In the final scene of Ian Fleming's novel "From Russia, With Love," Agent 007 is **stabbed** with a stiletto **dabbed** with **secretions** from the ovaries of a Japanese globefish, and instantly **flops** to the floor, an apparent **goner.** (Fortunately for Britannia, Bond was revived in the opening pages of the sequel, "Dr. No.")

The real world, alas is not so kind. On average, 100 Japanese a year are severely poisoned after indulging in this piscine favorite. About 30 die.

The most famous victim was Mitsugoro Bando, a Kabuki actor so revered that the government had designated him a Living National Treasure.

In January 1975, Bando swaggered into his favorite fugu restaurant in Kyoto and demanded a serving of sliced raw fugu liver. If the liver is washed and eaten in small quantities, the remnant toxin "produces a delightful sense of **numbness** of the mouth and extremities," according to a food column that appeared in the Yomiuri Shimbun, Japan's largest newspaper.

Delightful numbness notwithstanding, licensed fugu chefs are forbidden by law from serving the liver or other **lethal** portions of the globefish, no matter how much the paying public might clamor to play Nippon's version of **Russian roulette.** But this was no ordinary bon vivant. This was a genuine, in-the-flesh Living National Treasure, feeling very "nihon teki"—full of true Japanese spirit—what was more Japanese than a platter of **toxic** fish organs.

The chef **relented.** Bando tweezered sliver after **sliver** of fugu liver into his mouth with chopsticks. "Heavenly!" he declared. He then died horribly of convulsions followed by respiratory paralysis.

One might think the Japanese would take the actor's sad fate as an object lesson and leave the fugu to flipper happily unhindered through the deep.

But no.

"Japanese have a gambling spirit and enjoy good fish," said Hideyo Kimura, a city official in Shimonoseki, whose fishing fleet harvests 90 percent of the 2,200 tons of fugu that the Japanese consume annually. "People regard eating fugu as very sophisticated, very glamorous."

Reprinted from the *Boston Globe,* January 28, 1992.

Blowfish—*fugu* in Japanese—swim in a fish tank in a restaurant in Japan. The nonpoisonous flesh of the *fugu* is prized as a delicacy by the Japanese. (REUTERS/Susumu Takahashi/Archive photos.)

And they pay handsomely for their piscivorous treat.

A single serving of fugu sashimi, or raw fugu—the flesh sliced to paper-thin translucence and then artfully arranged in the shape of a flower or a crane—will **set the gourmand back** about $250. Fugu is also served in a sort of stew or as deep-fried tempura. "Eating fugu is a sort of extreme of the Japanese culture," said Tomoaki Nakao, director of the Shimonoseki Karato Uoichiba Co. Ltd., a huge wholesaler and retailer of fish, crabs, mollusks, squid, octopi and nearly every other underwater creature. Including, of course, fugu.

"There are more than 22 edible species of globefish," he said. "The more poisonous, the more popular."

Most poisonous and, thus, most prized of all is torafugu, or tigerfish, named for its distinctive orange stripes. Many is the bold diner who has tasted of the tora, smacked his lips in satisfaction, and then heaved a startled gasp, eyes rolling backward, chopsticks slipping from numbed hand.

The globefish species most avidly eaten by the Japanese are caught in the Yellow Sea and the East China Sea, as well as in waters around the southern island of Kyushu. Catching the fish is hazardous in itself.

"Shimonoseki fishermen catch nearly all Japan's fugu because only the fishermen of Shimonoseki are brave enough," said Akito Kamita, who, not surprisingly, is a fisherman of Shimonoseki. The city of 260,000 inhabitants is located on the Kanmon Strait between Kyushu and the main Japanese island of Honshu.

Fugu are snared on long lines rigged with hundreds of hooks and then **hauled** aboard and removed from the barb by hand. Fishermen have died after being pricked by a hook that has pierced a poisonous part of the fugu.

"Globefish are most popular to eat in January because the new year makes people feel expansive and lucky," Nakao said.

Sanpei Hiraoka, director of public health in Shimonoseki, insisted that eating fugu is perfectly safe—provided the chef is properly licensed and trained. Before earning the right to prepare and serve fugu without supervision, an aspiring fugu chef must undergo a three-year apprenticeship and then pass a rigorous series of tests and written examinations.

"It is almost like being a doctor, only we perform just one operation," said Kazuo Sasaki as he deftly excised the poisonous innards of a **plump** torafugu before turning the razor-sharp "hocho" blade to the sexual organs.

For the Japanese, fugu is not mere seafood to be consumed with no more thought than one might give to such ho-hum pedestrian **fare** as dried salt squid, **wriggling** live shrimp—called dancing ebi—or bright orange gobs of raw sea urchin roe.

"Eating fugu is an act of passion," Nakao said.

Indeed, fugu has seized the imagination of Japanese poets for centuries, although the traditional haiku and senryu verses inspired by the globefish tend toward the gloomy. As in Yosa Buson's celebrated poem of love lost:

I cannot see her tonight,
I have to give her up,
So I will eat fugu.

Once the eating of fugu was a crime in Japan. In 1590, the warlord Hideyoshi Toyotomi, enraged when his plans to do battle with a rival daimio had to be postponed after large numbers of his samurai died or became severely ill from feasting on fugu, **banned** consumption of the fish throughout the **realm.**

The edict was largely ignored, and by the mid-1600s the fish was popular among courtiers of the Tokugawa shogunate as well as sumo wrestlers, who asserted that when the fish did not kill it gave extra strength.

"Ever since the Edo period, fugu has been considered a gourmet dish even when it was technically illegal," said Kimura, whose office in the Shimonoseki municipal building is decorated with fugu balloons, fugu pottery, fugu ashtrays and posters depicting various species of fugu.

The legal ban was lifted in 1889. No one is certain why, although local legend has it that Prime Minister Hirobumi Ito paid a visit to Shimonoseki and was accidentally served globefish, which, law-abiding stalwart that he was, he had never before sampled.

"When informed the fish was fugu, the prime minister said that it was unforgivable that such a delicious taste should be prohibited," Kimura insisted. "So he ended the law, bringing great happiness to Japanese."

⫸ iBT Preparation

Independent Speaking Task

Students sit in two rows, facing each other. One row asks the questions, and the other row responds. The responders will have 15 to 30 seconds (teacher will decide time allotment) to prepare a response of 45 to 60 seconds. Questioners will be given a question on a piece of paper. They must not read the question; they must ask it in their own words. When the conversation between questioners and responders is finished, the responders move to the chair to their left and repeat the exercise with a new partner. The second time responders speak, there will be no preparation time.

Integrated Speaking Task

Read the following passage, and then listen to the passage that the teacher will read. Take notes on both. The teacher will also read a question. You will have 30 seconds to prepare your response. Again, speakers and listeners are in two rows. This time, the speakers respond only once, then roles are switched.

> *Economically, institutionalized gambling makes no sense. No wealth is created. Gambling simply involves the transfer of wealth from a lucky or smart person to an unlucky or foolish person. Gambling results in lower labor productivity and adds to **white-collar** crime. It adds to policing costs and to the costs that arise from drunk driving. There is also the problem of creating gambling addicts.*

The International View

What similar things are banned in your country? What things are permitted that some people think should be banned?

Paternalism in Action: American Laws

Objectives

- to understand that an abstraction like paternalism has very real consequences, because it is translated into laws that have penalties for violation

- to build a consensus

- to understand better the political culture of the United States

- to understand and employ the *principle of charity* in persuasive writing and oral argument

Introduction

A list of paternalistic laws that Americans disagree on appears on page 64. In most states of the United States, these laws are in effect. But the United States does have a rebellious history. The state of Massachusetts nearly had a revolution when a law was passed requiring motorists to wear seat belts. The people spoke up and, as in 1776, forced the law to be **repealed**. The majority of the people didn't want anybody to interfere with their right to choose, regardless of the fact that using seat belts was seen as a good thing.

As of 2007, 25 states do require drivers and passengers in cars to wear seat belts. They argue that it costs about $5,000 more per accident victim for hospital care for people who did not wear seat belts than for those who did. Altogether, the extra cost per state is about $10 million annually. This is paid by insurance companies, who pass on the costs to citizens by raising the price of insurance premiums. Of course, these states also cite statistics that show that seat belts save lives.

What do you think? *Should we be required to wear seat belts in cars, or should that be the choice of the people in the car?*

Vocabulary Gloss

repealed   = taken back, abolished (referring to laws)

consenting = agreeing

dueling   = formal combat between two persons using
                 weapons, with witnesses

Procedure

Put a check mark in the appropriate space to indicate whether you *agree* or *disagree* with the laws. Discuss these laws in small groups, and try to reach a consensus. When your group has finished its discussion, write a C in either the Agree column or the Disagree column to note where the group consensus was. See the explanatory notes for Questions 4, 5, 6, 7, and 8 on page 65.

    Agree   *Disagree*

1. ____ ____ laws requiring motorcyclists to wear safety helmets when driving

2. ____ ____ laws forbidding persons from swimming at a public beach when a lifeguard is not present

3. ____ ____ laws making suicide a crime

4. ____ ____ laws regulating certain kinds of sexual conduct among **consenting** adults in private

5. ____ ____ laws requiring a license to practice certain professions

6. ____ ____ laws forcing people to save a specified portion of their income for retirement (American Social Security system)

7. ____ ____ laws forbidding certain kinds of gambling

8. ____ ____ laws regulating the maximum rates of interest for loans

9. ____ ____ laws against **dueling**

Explanatory Notes

Question 4. In other words, can two adults, of any sex, draw the curtains in their own house and have any kind of sex they want, or can some sexual practices be banned because they are considered immoral?

Question 5. You have to have a license to practice medicine or law, for example. Can one person say to another person who is sick, "Look, I can make you better, and I will charge you one-tenth of what a doctor will charge, but you must understand I don't have a license."

Question 6. In the United States, approximately 8 percent of an employee's pay is automatically deducted and kept for retirement. You don't have any choice in this. You cannot say, "I'll invest in my retirement fund by myself, thank you." If you never stop working, you never get any of your money back. And you get it in monthly payments, so you might recover only a small fraction of what you pay in before you die.

Question 7. Betting on horse races is legal, and most lotteries are run by the state. You can gamble legally (roulette, card games, dice) in casinos in Las Vegas, Atlantic City, on some Native American reservations, and other places, but not everywhere.

Question 8. Loaning money at very high rates of interest (such as 50 percent) is called *loansharking*. Individuals who cannot get a loan from a bank often borrow money from *loansharks*—people who are willing to take a big risk and who may break your legs if you don't pay back on time. This money is often borrowed to pay for gambling debts.

Writing Assignment

Choose one of the paternalism issues (1–9), and write your opinion in defense of paternalism or of individual liberty. This is a philosophical argument, so address the arguments of the other side with the *principle of charity* in mind. The principle of charity in a philosophical argument means that you consider only the strongest argument contrary to yours. If you can destroy the strongest opposing arguments, the weaker ones will automatically fall. Write one page.

The International View

Are there laws in your country that you think are too paternalistic? Does your country lack laws that you think, paternalistically, should exist?

Does your country require the use of seat belts in cars?

JFK Memorial Hospital versus Heston

Objectives

- to learn the facts of a case for retelling, as is done in law schools

- to understand how a state supreme court decides a complicated case on paternalism and individual rights

Introduction

The following case was decided by the New Jersey Supreme Court. It is very relevant to the issue of "the right to die," which is much in the news. The case also deals with the very difficult issue of what to do when the right to practice one's own religion without government interference runs up against the right to life.

> ## Vocabulary Gloss
>
> **ruptured spleen** = broken organ near stomach
>
> **Jehovah's Witnesses** = a religious group
>
> **disoriented** = feeling lost or confused
>
> **incoherent** = unable to express thought clearly or logically
>
> **liability** = (legal) responsibility

Procedure

As you read and reflect, keep in mind John Stuart Mill's thesis and the arguments for paternalism. Collaborate in retelling the story, making sure that no important details have been omitted. Discuss the issue in small groups, with each person giving his or her viewpoint. Finally, your teacher will tell you what the state supreme court decided.

JFK Memorial Hospital versus Heston

Delores Heston, 22 and single, was severely injured in a car accident. At the hospital it was determined that she would die if not operated on for a **ruptured spleen** and that she would die if blood transfusions were not given.

Delores and her parents were **Jehovah's Witnesses,** a religious group that forbids blood transfusions. She later insisted that at the hospital she told doctors of her refusal to accept blood. But doctors and nurses said she was in shock. She was, or soon became, **disoriented** and **incoherent.**

The hospital by law has to do all it can to save lives. If Delores had signed a release of **liability** for the hospital and the staff, the transfusions would not have been given. But she was unable to. Her mother did, however, sign a release. Her father could not be located.

The hospital asked the Superior Court to be appointed guardian for Delores, and the judge agreed. Now the hospital was free to give transfusions, without which they would not operate. They did, and Delores got well.

The case of Delores Heston is finished, so we can't argue about what to do there. However, the issue of forcing someone to have a transfusion to save his or her life is one we can discuss. Can we do this, in spite of the person's religious beliefs? Can we force a person not to let himself or herself die?

Write a brief answer here. Your teacher may ask you to write a longer essay on this topic.

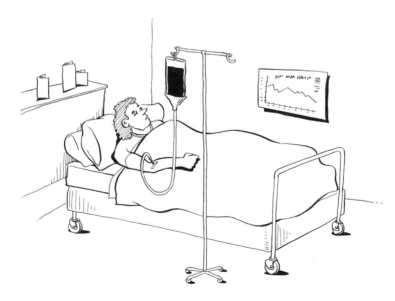

Can we force someone to have a transfusion
in spite of the person's religious beliefs?

⫸ iBT Preparation

Independent Speaking Task

Students sit in two rows, facing each other. One row asks the questions, and the other row responds. The responders will have 15 to 30 seconds (teacher will decide time allotment) to prepare a response of 45 to 60 seconds. Questioners will be given a question on a piece of paper. They must not read the question; they must ask it in their own words. When the conversation between questioners and responders is finished, the responders move to the chair to their left and repeat the exercise with a new partner. The second time responders speak, there will be no preparation time.

Integrated Speaking Task

Read the following passage, and then listen to the passage that the teacher will read. Take notes on both. The teacher will also read a question. You will have 30 seconds to prepare your response. Again, speakers and listeners are in two rows. This time, the speakers respond only once, then roles are switched.

> *Scientists are discovering enormous lakes under deserts in Africa and Australia. In the province of Victoria in Australia, there is a lake as big as Ireland under the desert. The water is at least 500 meters down in the ground. One problem is getting the water out of the ground. It may be worth the investment to try because the area is so dry. The biggest city, Perth, has been getting only 40 percent of average rainfall, so there is a desperate need to get more water.*

The International View

How does your country deal with the rights of religious minorities? Do groups like Jehovah's Witnesses exist? Do they face similar problems?

The Desert Dilemma

Objectives

- to make a decision that balances saving a life against the possibility of endangering others

- to practice *Conversation Cues* for *Adding Information* and *Pointing Out Irrelevancy*

Vocabulary Gloss

wide-brimmed	=	refers to a hat with a wide horizontal surface
uninhabited	=	no one lives there
oasis	=	water source in the desert, with vegetation
expedition	=	trip made by a group, often for scientific purposes

---

Procedure

Divide into two groups. The teacher will read essentially the same story to each group, separately, but with slight differences. Group I will have some facts that Group II does not have and vice versa. You will hear the story twice. The first time, just listen to familiarize yourself with the story. The second time, take notes (in English). This is not a dictation. Just write the important information, as you would in taking notes in a lecture.

Form small groups (preferably of four). Each group will have two people from Group I and two people from Group II.

Step 1

Retell the story, adding to the group's store of information. Make sure you have mentioned all the important facts and details. Use the information-adding expressions that follow.

Step 2

As you retell the story, listen for irrelevancies. Point them out as soon as you hear them. You will have a list of expressions to help you to do this (see page 72). A lot of deliberately irrelevant information was included in the story. You may disagree over the relevancy of some fact. This is fine. If your teacher hears some irrelevancy that is not noticed, he or she may hint at it.

Step 3

When you have pieced together the entire story, you must decide what to do. Use the map that follows to help you. Remember that *one* of you is among the people on the expedition! Your life depends on your decision. Find out if anyone has experience with the desert.

When you have reached a tentative decision, your teacher will comment on it. You may then wish to reconsider your decision. Finally, when all groups have finished, each will briefly tell its decision, and the others will comment on it.

Conversation Cues

Keep your book open to this page or write the cues on a separate piece of paper. Put a check mark next to a cue each time you use it.

Adding Information

May I add that . . .

I'd like to add something; . . .

One more thing we need to consider is . . .

I think it's important to add that . . .

I think it's important for us to know that . . .

We also need to take into account that . . .

Let's not forget that . . .

Pointing Out Irrelevancy

What does that have to do with it?

What does that have to do with our discussion?

What does that have to do with the topic?

I don't think that has anything to do with . . .

I don't think that is really related to . . .

How is that related to . . . ?

That really has nothing to do with what we're talking about.

I don't see how that fits into our discussion.

I fail to see the relevancy of_____ (that).

Is that really germane to our discussion?

Usage Note

Germane means "relevant."

Notes for the Desert Dilemma

⫸ iBT Preparation

Independent Speaking Task

Students sit in two rows, facing each other. The teacher will read the task. One row will be the speakers, and the other will be the listeners. The speakers will have 15 to 30 seconds (teacher will decide time allotment) to prepare a response of 45 to 60 seconds. When finished, speakers move to the desk immediately to the left and repeat the exercise with a new partner. When speakers have completed the task twice, they become the listeners, so that each student can speak twice. The second time speakers give their response, there will be no preparation time.

Integrated Speaking Task

Read the following passage, and then listen to the passage that the teacher will read. Take notes on both. The teacher will also read a question. You will have 30 seconds to prepare your response. Again, speakers and listeners are in two rows. This time, the speakers respond only once, then roles are switched.

> *If you are concerned about survival in the desert, it would be a good idea to look at the customs and dress of those who have lived in the desert. If you don't have a car, a camel is the best means of transportation. Camels can survive a long time without water. People who live in the desert wear long, loose-fitting clothing. Wearing something on your head is also crucial. A* ***wide-brimmed*** *hat is best.*

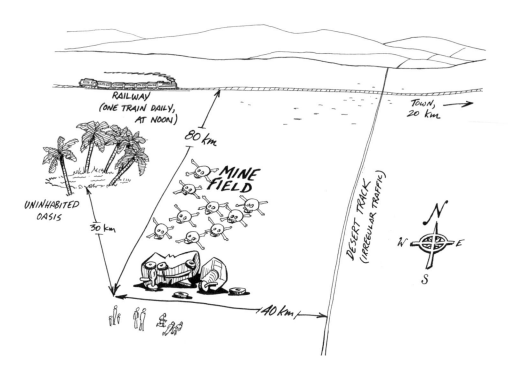

You are on an expedition to the Sahara Desert.

The International View

Do you know of any cases of survival in extreme circumstances? What happened?

Health Care: Rationing

Objectives

- to consider the ethical problem of rationing health care

- to write a policy paper

Introduction

One of the problems encountered by any country that wishes to provide health care for its citizens is rationing. With a finite amount of money, we have to make choices on how to spend it. Do we limit the number of services we will pay for, or do we limit the number of people who can get the services?

This is a difficult and a sad choice but an inevitable one. In England, for example, patients older than 75 years are denied **kidney dialysis.** The reason given is that the treatment is ineffective for that population. In the United States, on the other hand, rationing health care services is widely considered immoral, so we ration people. For example, anyone under the governmental health plan can get kidney dialysis, regardless of age, but many people are not poor enough to qualify for the plan. In other words, we give unlimited treatment to a small number of people. Other countries give limited treatment to a large number of people. Which philosophy is better? Whatever you decide, some kind of rationing will exist. In this unit, you will have to confront this difficult decision.

For example, let's say you have $1 million left in your health budget. You could spend it on either of the following.

a. Preventing death in 50 **elderly** people. This treatment would increase the quality of well-being (QWB) very little, and these people are expected to die within five years.

   or

b. Treatment for **acute arthritis** that would dramatically increase the QWB of 50,000 people and would last their lifetime (average age 45). Which would you choose?

Circle a or b. Discuss briefly in class. Of course, no one likes to make these kinds of choices, least of all politicians. We want to say a and b. So if you are unable to answer the question, that is okay.

Vocabulary Gloss

kidney dialysis = removing impurities from blood when kidneys don't function properly (frequent treatment)

elderly = old people

acute = severe

arthritis = inflammation of the joints

indigent = very poor

longevity = length of life, long life

rabies = disease usually transmitted by bites (fatal if untreated)

drowned = died in water

cramp = painful contraction of muscle, sometimes paralyzing

vegetable = (slang) person in a coma

resuscitation = being brought back from unconsciousness

updated = informed of latest news

cataracts = eye disease producing cloudy vision

appendectomy = operation to remove appendix

hepatitis = disease of the liver, causing fever and pain

diarrhea = illness in intestines bringing thin, watery feces

cholera = often fatal intestinal disease

maternity = pertaining to giving birth

Part 1. Values that Affect Health Care Rationing

We would like to have universal health care, but unfortunately we have limited funds. Thus, we need some criteria to help determine who and what conditions to treat.

A list of commonly agreed-on social health values—that is, reasons for giving treatment—that we can use to help decide our priorities follows. To make sure you understand these health values, find an example of each one.

Match the health value with an example of it (a–f). Put the correct letter in the answer blank.

_____ ability to function normally

_____ cost-effectiveness or cost-ineffectiveness

_____ length of life

_____ quality of life

_____ benefit to many as opposed to a few (value of system)

_____ equality of service (value of system)

a. expensive eye surgery allows me to see just 5 percent better

b. either free immunization shots for all kids *or* artificial hearts for 100 elderly

c. artificial lung machine

d. glasses

e. guaranteed access to all citizens

f. a wheelchair, medications

Part 2. Ranking Treatments as a Part of Health Care Rationing

Now apply these health values to some scenarios to see how they affect our decision making in creating a universal health plan with necessary rationing.

Suppose you (the class) are a committee charged with making a recommendation for spending a small amount of money on some **indigent** patients. Your boss orders you to come up with a ranking of who should get treatment. You know there is not enough money for treatment of all of the patients. You also know that the doctors and hospital staff in this place are underpaid and are angry about it; they will not work unless they get paid. (Sad but true.)

First, your boss asks you a question: "We have two possible criteria for providing treatment. Which should we choose?"

a. Should we treat whoever walked (or was carried) through the door first?

   or

b. Should we decide according to the benefit of the treatment (e.g., the person at the front of the line has a stomachache and the last person in line is bleeding badly, so treating the last person has more benefit)?

Choose a or b, then discuss in class.

Now the boss says, "Proceed on the basis that I have decided on b. Here is a list of patients demanding treatment. We do not have the funds to treat all of them today. Give me a prioritized treatment list. Who will be treated first, second, and so forth—put a number in the blank before the patient's name. I am not asking you to play God; I am just telling you that our minimal resources will prevent all from being treated. The taxpayers refuse to pay more money; they're already screaming about high taxes. Do your best and understand that the final decision rests with me. I have provided you with the cost level of each treatment [in brackets]. When you add up your total cost level, the costs must not exceed 13." (The total could be less.) Put a check mark on the line indicating which patients you have chosen.

To help make your decision, ask yourself the following question: What difference will treatment make, as opposed to no treatment (in terms of **longevity,** quality of life, ability to function normally)?

In class, meet in groups of three or four and make a consensus decision on who will be treated. Write the names of those you have chosen for treatment on the board. Compare your choices, comment on the other groups' choices, and defend your group's choices.

_____ Adam was bitten by a dog that he says was normally very friendly. The dog's appearance makes him suspect that it may have **rabies.** The dog has run off. Adam is afraid he caught rabies from the dog, and he wants shots to cure it. He is 13 and in this country illegally. *[cost level 1]*

_____ Betty has just learned that she is pregnant. Betty is a cocaine addict. She is worried that the baby will be born addicted, and she wants to enter a drug treatment program to break her addiction. She has tried to do it herself in the past and failed. The father-to-be of the child is unknown. She is 16. *[cost level 2]*

_____ Chad is in a coma after having nearly **drowned.** He climbed the fence around someone's swimming pool one night and got a **cramp** while swimming. A lung infection has set in. He needs very expensive treatment from a lung-bypass machine, and one doctor has guessed that he will probably be a **"vegetable"** even if he survives. The dramatic **resuscitation** of Chad was filmed by a TV crew and was seen by millions of people on the 7:00 news. The reporters said that they would keep the public **updated** on Chad's condition. He is 12. *[cost level 5]*

_____ Dolores has unclear vision due to **cataracts** and needs operations on both eyes. Her only pleasure in life, she says, is reading, and now she can't do that. If untreated, the cataracts could cause blindness. She is 62. *[cost level 3]*

_____ Eulalia needs kidney dialysis on a continuing basis or she will die. She is 50. *[cost level 5]*

_____ Frank has severe arthritis in his hands and wants drugs and physical therapy to control it. He makes his living by playing piano at cheap bars. He is 40. *[cost level 2]*

_____ Gary, 25, is blind and wants a seeing-eye dog. *[cost level 1]*

_____ Ida has AIDS and wants a drug that will prolong her life by about five years. Without it, she'll die in six months. She is 35 and is the mother of two healthy children, ages two and four. *[cost level 2]*

_____ Humbert has a broken hip (the result of chasing after women, it is alleged). With treatment, there is a 98 percent chance he'll have full recovery. Without treatment, there is a 90 percent chance that he will be unable to walk. He is 61. *[cost level 3]*

_____ John needs an **appendectomy.** He is 90 and has a life expectancy of one year if the operation is successful. *[cost level 3]*

Writing Assignment

Top executives must make policy decisions, and these can be very difficult to make. Your assignment here is one of the hardest. Suppose that the United States is restructuring its health care system. You have enough money in the health care budget to care for the majority of patients, but not all. Some sort of rationing must occur. The President of the United States wants a policy to be distributed to all the hospitals in the country. You must write this policy. The President asks you, "How do we spend the fixed amount of health care money? How do we decide whom to spend it on? Shall we just give health care to everybody who wants it, then when all the money is gone, in maybe six months, close down the hospitals?" Using the exercise on pages 79–80 as a starting point, write a policy paper of approximately two pages.

One student in each group will not write this paper, for he or she is the President. The President will read all the papers and then will write comments to each of the students, telling the students what ideas appeared good and what each policy paper was lacking (if anything).

Health Care: Providing Services to Visible and Invisible Victims

Objectives

- to consider cost-effectiveness for the health care system in general

- to write a speech

- to speak persuasively

Introduction

Previously you discussed cost-effectiveness for individual treatments but not for the system in general. However, this consideration is extremely important. For example, one of the best things a city can do to improve and ensure the health of its citizens is to put in a water purification plant. This provides incalculable benefits in reducing pain and productivity loss from stomach viruses, **hepatitis, diarrhea,** and even **cholera.**

Ironically, cost-effectiveness is often ignored in the United States because the victims are invisible. It can be proven statistically that if we provide **maternity** care before, during, and after birth, many lives will be saved. But those who don't get this care are nameless, statistical victims. On the other hand, when a two-year-old gets stuck in a pipe and the national news networks cover the story, we will spend any amount to restore the child to health. We like to see ourselves as charitable people, and helping such a child reaffirms our social values. In addition, not spending the money might be political suicide for elected officials.

We will investigate this issue with a writing assignment based on the earlier case of Chad.

Chad is in a coma after having nearly drowned. He climbed the fence around someone's swimming pool one night and got a cramp while swimming. A lung infection has set in. He needs very expensive treatment from a lung-bypass machine, and one doctor has guessed that he will probably be a "vegetable" even if he survives. The dramatic resuscitation of Chad was filmed by a TV crew and was seen by millions of people on the 7:00 news. The reporters said that they would keep the public updated on Chad's condition. He is 12.

Chad climbed a fence around someone's swimming pool one night
and got a cramp while swimming.

To this we will add a few details.

Chad must be transferred from Florida to Minneapolis, Minnesota, where they
have a sophisticated lung machine. The experts now say that at best Chad will
be severely impaired. His brain was cut off from oxygen for too long. But with
life-support systems he could live a very long time, at tremendous expense. The
state of Florida has already paid $10,000 to keep him alive.

Chad has been on the front page of many newspapers, and tomorrow the
governor has a news conference in which it is certain that she will be asked
what the state plans to do about Chad.

Because of budget problems, major cities have recently cut back the number of police and firefighters, and they have been asking for aid to hire them
back. Revenues are down because the state is in a recession. The citizens
elected this governor because she promised no new taxes. Minority groups have
been asking the governor for $250,000 for maternity care and for free immu-
nizations for poor people. The governor has been delaying on this for a year, not
wanting to put the state further in debt. Keeping Chad alive will cost between
$100,000 and $500,000.

Writing Assignment

You are a speechwriter and advisor to the governor, and you get paid a lot of money for what you do. The governor has asked you to write a one-page speech on Chad that he will read at the news conference tomorrow. Write the speech.

Reading a Speech

Your teacher will choose three speeches that will be read by the authors in class. Students will be divided into three groups, and each group will help one author prepare his or her reading. Make sure that the reader

1. has good pace (not too slow, not too fast)

2. pauses after some important lines

3. forcefully stresses the important words and phrases

4. looks up to make occasional eye contact

5. uses hand gestures and/or other body language

Judging will be based on which speech you would choose if you were the governor. The judge will be (in order of preference) either someone who is not a class member, a selected student not participating in the preparation, or the teacher.

⫸ iBT Preparation

Independent Speaking Task

Students sit in two rows, facing each other. The teacher will read the task. One row will be the speakers, and the other will be the listeners. The speakers will have 15 to 30 seconds (teacher will decide time allotment) to prepare a response of 45 to 60 seconds. When finished, speakers move to the desk immediately to the left and repeat the exercise with a new partner. When speakers have completed the task twice, they become the listeners, so that each student can speak twice. The second time speakers give their response, there will be no preparation time.

Integrated Speaking Task

Read the following passage, and then listen to the passage that the teacher will read. Take notes on both. The teacher will also read a question. You will have 30 seconds to prepare your response. Again, speakers and listeners are in two rows. This time, the speakers respond only once, then roles are switched.

A major health concern in developing countries is dengue fever, which is transmitted by mosquitoes. Researchers, led by Dr. Jose Suaya at the Heller School of Brandeis University, are studying the impact of dengue and are trying to interest governments in financing research into a vaccine. One significant problem is that drug companies don't forecast large profits from such a vaccine because it would be administered largely to people who cannot afford it.

Knowledge, Information, and Ethics in Relation to Insurance and Health Care

Objective

- to consider the influence of ethics on insurance and health care

Introduction

Alexander Pope wrote, "A little knowledge is a dangerous thing." He meant that "a lot of" knowledge is preferable. But in our information age, perhaps that is not always so. We will now look at a few ethical problems that arise from our scientific and technological ability to learn much more about our health and to transmit this knowledge easily.

Not long ago, the Boston Transit Authority learned that one of its bus drivers was illiterate—unable to read. He had successfully driven a bus for years (we don't know how he got his driver's license) without any problems. He was an outstanding employee. He was fired. Was this right?

We will look at problems dealing with group and individual knowledge and try to decide what role knowledge and information should play in our decision making.

Vocabulary Gloss

bulk = in large quantities

Procedure

Decide whether your answer is yes or no in each case, and put a check mark next to your choice. In small groups, compare answers and explain why you made your choices and why you think they are best. Because these are hard questions, you may have doubts about what you think best. If so, explain your doubts to the group.

1. Men have more car accidents than women. Should men have to pay more in insurance premiums than women? This is sexual discrimination, but we already practice age discrimination in automobile insurance policies. If you are over age 65 or under age 21, you pay more simply by virtue of being young or old. But, of course, insurance companies sometimes frame the issue differently, saying that there is a "discount" for those over age 21 and under age 65.

   Yes _____   No _____

2. Women live longer than men. Should women receive a "discount" in life insurance? (The sooner you die, the sooner the company has to pay benefits.)

   Yes _____   No _____

3. I am a young man who likes skydiving, bungee jumping, whitewater canoeing, and a lot of other very dangerous activities. I seem to be addicted to risk, though I don't know why. The Cheathem Insurance Company does not want to sell me life insurance. Should they be forced to?

   Yes _____   No _____

4. My insurance company has learned that my parents smoked two packs of cigarettes a day apiece and that they both died of lung cancer at an early age. I don't smoke, but the insurance company wants either to exclude lung cancer from my policy or to make me pay 50 percent more to cover the risk. Should they be allowed to do this?

   Yes _____   No _____

5. My insurance company knows that I have a defect in a certain gene, which usually leads to cancer. I don't know how they got the information. They want to exclude cancer from my health insurance and from my life insurance or charge astronomically high premiums. Is this fair? (By the way, your father owns the insurance company!)

   Yes _____   No _____

⫸ iBT Preparation

Independent Speaking Task

Students sit in two rows, facing each other. The teacher will read the task. One row will be the speakers, and the other will be the listeners. The speakers will have 15 to 30 seconds (teacher will decide time allotment) to prepare a response of 45 to 60 seconds. When finished, speakers move to the desk immediately to the left and repeat the exercise with a new partner. When speakers have completed the task twice, they become the listeners, so that each student can speak twice. The second time speakers give their response, there will be no preparation time.

Integrated Speaking Task

Read the following passage, and then listen to the passage that the teacher will read. Take notes on both. The teacher will also read a question. You will have 30 seconds to prepare your response. Again, speakers and listeners are in two rows. This time, the speakers respond only once, then roles are switched.

> *Perhaps the biggest socioeconomic problem the United States faces today is the skyrocketing costs of health care. One easy way to control the cost of drugs is to negotiate lower prices for **bulk** purchases. Discounts for bulk purchases are the American way of doing business, but they are illegal when it comes to Medicare, the government program for people over age 65.*

Psychology

Survey

Objectives

- to establish a quantitative view of marriage in the United States
- to interact with native speakers
- to increase cross-cultural awareness

Introduction

In some courses, particularly psychology, you will be required to survey the population at large. You will be surprised at how often the quantitative facts are different from your expectations.

> ### Vocabulary Gloss
>
> **sustain** = to support the weight of, keep up
>
> **openness** = telling the truth, not hiding things

Procedure

Fill out the survey. Then ask one to five native speakers the same questions. Whenever possible, just read them the question and the list of responses. If their answers surprise you, ask them why they responded as they did. In class, the teacher will conduct an informal poll of responses, and you will have a chance to comment on what surprised you and on any situations in which things are much different in your country. The teacher will give you the correct answers.

1. Between _____ of all Americans get married at least once.

   a. 90 and 95 percent
   b. 80 and 90 percent
   c. 70 and 80 percent

2. Within five years after a divorce, _____ Americans remarry.

   a. most
   b. about half of the
   c. few

3. _____ Americans marry more than twice.
   a. Many
   b. Few
   c. No

4. With regard to nonverbal behavior, _____ are better at reading facial expressions, and _____ are better at interpreting a spouse's tone of voice. [Fill in with *men* or *women*.]

5. Self-disclosure (revealing one's feelings) is more important
   a. at the beginning of a relationship
   b. further along in a relationship

6. Relationships are able to **sustain** total **openness** over long periods of time.
   a. yes
   b. no

7. *What do American couples argue about?* Rate these items by putting a number, 1–5, over each of them. 1 means most; 5 means least. The teacher will give you the correct answers. Remember, you are considering American couples, and the ranking order will not necessarily be the same as in your country. When you have the answers, discuss with your teacher the differences and similarities in ranking order for different stages of marriage. (*Note:* Good communication will prevent your spouse from feeling and saying things like, "You don't talk to me enough" and "Why didn't you tell me that?")

   a. early in marriage

      relatives   money   sex   communication   jealousy

   b. early parenthood

      relatives   money   sex   communication   jealousy

   c. later on—around 15 years to end

      relatives   money   sex   communication   jealousy

8. How much time do married couples living together actually spend talking to each other per week?

   a. less than ½ hour

   b. 1 hour

   c. 5 hours

   d. 10 hours

9. What percentage of American families have dinner together (all present) regularly?

   a. 10 percent

   b. 40 percent

   c. 60 percent

   d. 75 percent

The International View

In your country, do couples argue about different issues from the ones given in this section? Would the order of what they argue most about be substantially different?

Marriage, Cross-Culturally

Objectives

- to clarify what marriage is
- to share cross-cultural perspectives on marriage and what a good spouse is

Introduction

Marriage is not only a topic you will explore in this chapter on psychology, but something you will need at least to consider seriously. Begin by sharing what you think about marriage.

Procedure

Check the items that you agree with. In small groups, discuss which you chose and which you did not choose and why. Space is left for you to add items that you think are important and that have been omitted. Mention these to your group.

Part 1. Marriage Is about . . .

_____	sharing as much time as possible together
_____	romance
_____	keeping separate identities, activities, and interests
_____	sharing innermost feelings, both positive and negative
_____	having a good time
_____	a lifetime commitment
_____	being faithful
_____	_____
_____	_____
_____	_____
_____	_____

Part 2. Characteristics of a Good Spouse

As a class, make suggestions to generate a list of 15 characteristics of a good spouse. *Spouse* does not refer to just wife or husband, but both! And the characteristics should not apply just to a spouse you want but to all good spouses. When the full list is on the board, copy it. Meet in small groups and form a consensus list of the 10 most important characteristics of a good spouse. In other words, your group must decide to eliminate five of the characteristics that the class generated. Cross out the ones your group eliminates. If you are strongly opposed to a characteristic being on the list, you may insist that it be removed. The consensus list must be acceptable to everyone. When you are done, the groups should report to the class as a whole on which characteristics they eliminated. Other groups may comment on the choices.

Characteristics of a Good Spouse

_____

_____

_____

_____

_____

_____

_____

_____

_____

_____

_____

_____

_____

_____

⫸ iBT Preparation

Independent Speaking Task

Students sit in two rows, facing each other. The teacher will read the task. One row will be the speakers, and the other will be the listeners. The speakers will have 15 to 30 seconds (teacher will decide time allotment) to prepare a response of 45 to 60 seconds. When finished, speakers move to the desk immediately to the left and repeat the exercise with a new partner. When speakers have completed the task twice, they become the listeners, so that each student can speak twice. The second time speakers give their response, there will be no preparation time.

Integrated Speaking Task

Read the following passage, and then listen to the passage that the teacher will read. Take notes on both. The teacher will also read a question. You will have 30 seconds to prepare your response. Again, speakers and listeners are in two rows. This time, the speakers respond only once, then roles are switched.

> *What most people know about Islam is that polygamy, having more than one wife, is practiced. Moslem men are permitted to have four wives at any one time. But there are other aspects of matrimony that people should know. For instance, the prophet said, "Marry women that are loving and fertile." The prophet also said, "A woman is married for four reasons: her wealth, her lineage, her beauty, and her religion. So choose the woman with good religious qualities."*

Gender Attitudes: A Compatibility Survey

This exercise is to be done in a mixed-sex class.

"Gender attitudes" refers to the attitudes that we have toward roles of men and women in a culture. These attitudes are a good predictor of marital satisfaction. That is, if you and your partner have similar attitudes, you are more likely to be a happy couple. If you and your partner have very different attitudes, you are less likely to be a happy couple in the long run.

In this exercise you will compare your attitudes with those of a student (or students) of the opposite sex. Remember that sharing similar attitudes about important matters will help two people have a happy marriage.

Vocabulary Gloss

long range = for 10 or 20 years

achiever = person who earns the money, honors, makes a reputation

worse off = not doing so well (psychologically, physically, mentally)

egalitarians = people believing in equality

gay = (slang) homosexual

Procedure

A list of questions on page 96 will be used to test your compatibility with a partner. For each question, circle the response that is closest to your own beliefs: *St. Ag.* = strongly agree; *Ag.* = agree; *Dis.* = disagree; *St. Dis.* = strongly disagree.

Compatibility Questions

1. A working mother can establish just as warm and secure a relationship with her children as a mother who does not work.

   St. Ag.   Ag.   Dis.   St. Dis.

2. Parents should encourage just as much independence in their daughters as in their sons.

   St. Ag.   Ag.   Dis.   St. Dis.

3. Men should share the housework, such as doing the dishes, cleaning, and so forth, with women.

   St. Ag.   Ag.   Dis.   St. Dis.

4. Men and women should be paid the same money if they do the same work.

   St. Ag.   Ag.   Dis.   St. Dis.

5. Women should be considered as seriously as men for jobs as executives or politicians or President.

   St. Ag.   Ag.   Dis.   St. Dis.

6. A man can make **long range** plans for his life, but a woman can deal only with day-to-day problems.

   St. Ag.   Ag.   Dis.   St. Dis.

7. It is more important for a wife to help her husband's career than to have a career herself.

   St. Ag.   Ag.   Dis.   St. Dis.

8. It is much better for everyone involved if the man is the **achiever** outside the home and the woman takes care of the home and family.

   St. Ag.   Ag.   Dis.   St. Dis.

9. A preschool child will probably be **worse off** if his or her mother works.

   St. Ag.   Ag.   Dis.   St. Dis.

10. Women who do not want at least one child are being selfish.

    St. Ag.   Ag.   Dis.   St. Dis.

For each question, compare your choice with a partner of the opposite sex. If there are unequal numbers of males and females, you may have to compare with two partners. First, put a check mark to indicate your opinion under one of the four choices in the Compatibility Rating chart. Then mark your partner's choice. Discuss the reasons for your decisions. Then, using these guidelines, put a number (0–3) in the compatibility column of the Compatibility Rating chart.

    a. If you and your partner have the same response, put 0.

    b. If your responses are adjacent (e.g., *strongly agree/agree*, or *agree/disagree*, or *disagree/strongly disagree*), put 1.

    c. If your responses are two apart, (e.g., *agree/strongly disagree*), put 2.

    d. If your responses are three apart (e.g., *strongly agree/strongly disagree*), put 3.

When you finish discussing all the gender attitudes statements, total your compatibility score. The lower the score, the more compatible you and your partner are.

    As a group, you might want to find out who had the lowest and highest scores. You might also enjoy finding out how many **egalitarians** and how many traditionalists there are in your class. Is one gender more traditional than the other?

Compatibility Rating Compatibility Number	St. Ag.	Ag.	Dis.	St. Dis.
1. ____	____	____	____	____
2. ____	____	____	____	____
3. ____	____	____	____	____
4. ____	____	____	____	____
5. ____	____	____	____	____
6. ____	____	____	____	____
7. ____	____	____	____	____
8. ____	____	____	____	____
9. ____	____	____	____	____
10. ____	____	____	____	____

Egalitarian [ ]   *Traditional* [ ]

Look at your own responses for numbers 1–5. If you agreed or strongly agreed with most of them, you are an *egalitarian*. Put a check mark in the box.

Check your responses for numbers 6–10. If you agreed or strongly agreed with most of these, you are *traditional*. Put a check mark in the box.

⫸ iBT Preparation

Independent Speaking Task

Students sit in two rows, facing each other. The teacher will read the task. One row will be the speakers, and the other will be the listeners. The speakers will have 15 to 30 seconds (teacher will decide time allotment) to prepare a response of 45 to 60 seconds. When finished, speakers move to the desk immediately to the left and repeat the exercise with a new partner. When speakers have completed the task twice, they become the listeners, so that each student can speak twice. The second time speakers give their response, there will be no preparation time.

Integrated Speaking Task

Read the following passage, and then listen to the passage that the teacher will read. Take notes on both. The teacher will also read a question. You will have 30 seconds to prepare your response. Again, speakers and listeners are in two rows. This time, the speakers respond only once, then roles are switched.

> *One of the issues the United States is facing is **gay** marriage, but just to mention the issue is to frame it in a way that has political appeal for either liberals or conservatives. "Gay" is a victory for liberals because the alternative "homosexual marriage" sounds worse. How an issue is framed turns out to be very important in determining how people will think about it. But conservatives have won most of the language wars. They have spent millions of dollars investigating how to win language wars.*

Marital Issues

Objectives

- to find out to what extent the class agrees on the issues of ideology, interdependence, and communication in marriage

- to explore cross-cultural attitudes on these issues

- to share wedding customs

- to practice planning a low-cost wedding

Part 1: "Of Love and Money"

Read the article, and be prepared to answer the discussion questions in class. The article will stimulate your thinking on how money becomes an issue where love is usually the priority. You should be thinking about whether the Egyptian experience of marriage is similar to yours. If your classmates are from different countries, find out if they have problems similar to those encountered by the Egyptians.

Vocabulary Gloss

dowry	= money or property given from the groom's family to the bride
gap	= distance between two points
ostentatious	= show of wealth to impress people
conspicuous	= easily visible
chic	= stylish or elegant
elite	= small group of powerful people
frivolous	= silly and trivial
lavish	= extravagant
crippling	= debilitating, reducing ability to do something
fallout	= undesirable consequences (radioactive dust from nuclear explosion)

Of Love and Money

By G. Willow Wilson

Twenty-one-year-old Zayna lives with her family in a lower-middle-class area of Giza. It's a neighborhood where streets are not always paved and are often marred by puddles of sewage; where the majority of residents work low-paying government jobs or run small grocery stores. Today, Zayna and her family are celebrating: she is about to be engaged. The groom-to-be and his family shake hands all around with Zayna's parents and family and seat themselves in the main room. His father presents her with a jewelry box, inside which is her *shabka*: a gold ring set with six diamonds, worth about LE 20,000 [$3,000 USD]. The word 'shabka' shares a common root with the verb 'to tie', and it is generally believed that this traditional gift of expensive jewelry from the groom's family is meant to bind the young couple, placing them under a social and financial obligation to one another. Though the ring is worth as much as her parents earn in a year, it is not an extravagant bridal gift by modern Egyptian standards. The family of a middle-class groom can now expect to pay up to LE 15,000 for the dowry of a middle-class girl—LE 15,000 for her **dowry,** plus an additional LE 60,000 to 70,000 for the apartment where the young couple will live. In turn, a bride's family is expected to throw a large wedding, which can cost anywhere between LE 10,000 and LE 30,000; and to furnish the apartment, which often costs at least that amount again. The financial strain of marriage plunges many families into debt for years.

Thirty years ago, many Egyptian women refused to accept large dowries; today the **gap** between rich and poor is widening, but expensive dowries have staged a dramatic comeback. The reasons why may be surprising. "This is **ostentatious** consumption," says Pascale Ghazaleh, who teaches Middle Eastern history at the American University in Cairo. "Not **conspicuous** consumption. Something else is at work. Even today, in families that consider themselves educated and 'Old Money', it's shameful for a woman to accept more than the minimum [for a dowry]." The minimum amount a groom is required by law to give his bride as a dowry is a single Egyptian pound.

Large dowries mean more pressure on young unmarried men, a segment of Egyptian society already economically challenged by the country's high rate of unemployment. Jobs in government bureaucracy, traffic policing and manual labor pay as little as LE 400 per month; even with supplementary income, many Egyptian men cannot afford to marry before their mid-thirties. The explanations they give for the recent upward trend in dowries are increasingly pessimistic. "People imitate the upper classes," says Mostafa, a floor manager in a local paint factory. Mostafa is twenty-five and trying to save up enough money to marry within a year. "I'm angry," he says, "I could get married in a few months with a good flat and furnishings, but because of the expenses of the dowry, I have to wait. It doubles my expenses. People demand these things because they want to appear **chic** and well-off. Now it's a must: since most people in the middle classes ask for these things, everyone must ask for these things."

Mohammad, a twenty-six-year-old classical musician, is even more emphatic. "It's a form of prostitution," he says. "Pretty girls are worth more than ugly girls. Educated girls are worth more than uneducated girls. It was the same way in the slave markets two hundred years ago. Nothing has changed."

While imitation of the wealthy **elite** may indeed account for the market price of the modern dowry, there are those who believe the trend toward extravagance has a religious element. "Part of the problem comes from returnees from the Gulf," says Sohair, a single mother who is helping her youngest son save money for his marriage. "Society has become religious in a very rigid way," she says. "People are not free to enjoy themselves in public, so they live very limited, domestic lives—expensive furniture, big weddings, jewelry, these are the things that are important to them, because they have no outside life. Everything has become *haram* [forbidden]."

Muslim authorities, however, contradict the theory that rising dowry and wedding costs are connected to rising levels of religious conservatism. An Al Azhar scholar, who wished to have his name withheld, put forth another explanation. "This extravagance is due to a lack of integrity among the youth," he said. "A father wants to secure his daughter's future and reputation. Today, this is only possible if a potential groom is tied to his fiancée financially. Modern young men and women don't like having

responsibilities. If a young man has invested nothing in his future bride, he might abandon the engagement when he gets tired of it, leaving the girl with a compromised reputation. So parents ask for large dowries to protect their daughters from young men with **frivolous** intentions."

Dowry-giving is part of Islamic law: for devout Muslims, a marriage cannot take place without one. "*Mahr* [dowry or bride-price] is the sum of money or other property which the husband agrees to pay to his bride on or shortly after the marriage. It becomes her property, and is hers to keep if the marriage ends in divorce," says Ruqaiyyah Waris Maqsood, former chair of the GCSE Islamic Studies program in Britain. According to scholars like Maqsood, the **lavish** weddings and expensive marital settlements that occur today in many parts of the Muslim world fly in the face of Islamic law, despite the insistence of many Muslims that these outlays of money are a religious necessity. "Financially **crippling** celebrations are totally in opposition to the spirit of Islam, and are not necessary," says Maqsood. "They are purely a matter of the culture of certain regions. No Muslim should feel obliged to continue these unIslamic traditions, or be embarrassed about breaking with their old cultural traditions."

This does not seem likely to happen soon in Egypt. Whether the skyrocketing expense of marriage is rooted in imitation of the wealthy elite, psychological **fallout** from the revival of religion or youthful frivolity, it seems as though it is here to stay.

Discussion Questions

Are weddings in your country as extravagant? Do they cost as much as in Egypt? Do you have the custom of dowry?

Part 2: Wedding Planners

Zadie and Farouq are friends you met while studying at the University of Michigan. Now you have all graduated and they intend to get married in Las Vegas rather than in Cairo, avoiding the traditional expensive wedding, the dowry, etc. But they still cannot afford the estimated costs. Because you are professional wedding planners, they have asked you to reduce the allocation of money for various items in a way that will be tolerable to most people and will still leave everybody happy with the wedding. Remember: these are your close friends; you want their wedding to be memorable. Decide yourself the new cost of each item. Then discuss in groups and come up with a consensus. Most important, you must tell in detail what you would do to reduce the expense; for example, "She should borrow my sister's wedding gown; then it won't cost her anything." Total the consensus costs. Compare your total reduction with that of other groups. The lowest cost is the winner. Teacher may give you M&Ms or some small prize.

Item	Estimated Cost ($)	New Estimated Cost
1. Invitations, thank you notes, announcements	200	_____
2. Bridal gown and accessories	2,000	_____
3. Flowers and floral decorations & corsages	2,300	_____
4. Photographs and video of wedding	1,500	_____
5. Musicians and singer for wedding	900	_____
6. Band for reception	2,000	_____
7. Transportation and lodging for out of town guests	1,500	_____
8. Bridesmaids luncheon	300	_____
9. Rental of reception hall at country club	1,000	_____
10. Gifts for bridesmaids and groom's attendants	200	_____
11. Ties and gloves for groom's attendants	300	_____
12. Wedding rehearsal dinner for 16 people	1,500	_____
13. Wedding bands (rings)	700	_____
14. Reception (sit-down dinner, free bar, 100 guests)	10,000	_____
15. Groom's tuxedo and accessories	1,000	_____
16. Wedding cake	300	_____
17. Honeymoon (5 nights in Acapulco)	2,000	_____
Total	**$27,700**	_____

⫸ iBT Preparation

Independent Speaking Task

Students sit in two rows, facing each other. The teacher will read the task. One row will be the speakers, and the other will be the listeners. The speakers will have 15 to 30 seconds (teacher will decide time allotment) to prepare a response of 45 to 60 seconds. When finished, speakers move to the desk immediately to the left and repeat the exercise with a new partner. When speakers have completed the task twice, they become the listeners, so that each student can speak twice. The second time speakers give their response, there will be no preparation time.

Integrated Speaking Task

Read the following passage, and then listen to the passage that the teacher will read. Take notes on both. The teacher will also read a question. You will have 30 seconds to prepare your response. Again, speakers and listeners are in two rows. This time, the speakers respond only once, then roles are switched.

> *Mrs. Nasser was determined to limit the cost of her daughter's wedding. She cancelled plans for the traditional belly dancers and the twenty-piece band that were going to accompany her daughter's entrance to the reception in the grand ball room of the Alexandria Hilton Hotel. Instead, she chose to have a reception with fewer guests at their favorite Mexican restaurant with a four-piece mariachi band. She also cancelled the life-size ice sculptures of the bride and the groom, all of which the groom's family had planned on.*

Part 3: Ideology, Interdependence, and Communication Issues

There is a correlation of successful marriage and similar views on ideology, interdependence, and communication.

Put a check mark in the blank indicating whether you agree (Ag.) or disagree (Dis.) with these 16 statements. In groups of three or four, discuss your responses to each statement. When you finish, share your best responses with members of the opposite sex. If you have almost the same answers, maybe you should get married.

	Ag.	Dis.
Ideology		
1. A woman should take her husband's last name when she marries.	_____	_____
2. My wedding ceremony will be (was) very important to me.	_____	_____
3. In marriage, fidelity is not necessary.	_____	_____
4. In the perfect relationship, there is much laughing and doing of things spontaneously (as soon as they come to mind).	_____	_____
Interdependence		
5. It is important for a couple to tell each other how much they care about and love each other.	_____	_____
6. When one spouse feels depressed or bad, the other spouse should comfort and reassure him or her.	_____	_____
7. It is important for one to have some private space that is all his or her own and separate from the spouse's.	_____	_____
8. One spouse should feel free to interrupt the other when he or she is concentrating on something and is in the same room.	_____	_____
9. It is okay to open your spouse's *personal* mail without asking permission.	_____	_____

10. One should feel free to invite guests home without informing one's spouse.   _____ _____

11. The main meal that the couple or family has together should be served at the same time every day.   _____ _____

Communication

12. Some problems will disappear if you avoid arguing about them.   _____ _____

13. In a relationship it is better to avoid conflicts than to engage in them.   _____ _____

14. It is better to hide one's true feelings in order to avoid hurting your spouse.   _____ _____

15. It is sometimes okay for one spouse to force the other to do things that he or she does not want to do.   _____ _____

16. It is usually okay to argue in front of friends or in public places.   _____ _____

Divorce

Objective

- to explore the criterion of *fault* in a just settlement following a divorce

Introduction

This investigation crosses several realms. You will become aware of gender differences in marital issues. No other issue divides the sexes in a classroom setting as clearly as the issue of property rights tends to. The reason may be that it hits people where, supposedly, it hurts most—in the wallet. In addition to looking at this issue in relation to psychology (the major topic of this chapter), we examined it in studying philosophy (Unit 2) and law (Unit 3).

Alimony is the money that one spouse pays the other as a result of divorce. Generally it goes from the husband to the wife. It can be a settlement (one-time large sum) or a monthly allowance that will continue until the recipient remarries. It does not include money for *child support*—that is a separate item, referring to payments for food, clothing, and other expenses that go along with raising children. Alimony is more like a living allowance. In some states it doesn't matter who is at fault in causing the divorce; in others, it does matter.

Introductory Question (Discuss)

To your knowledge, in your country does it matter who is at fault when determining how much money to award in alimony?

Vocabulary Gloss

amicably = in a friendly manner

virtually = practically, approximately

Procedure

Should *fault* be a factor in determining the amount of alimony? We will consider each of the following cases (a, b, c) one at a time. In small groups, decide how much, if anything, should be paid, per year. The teacher will write the decision of each group on the chalkboard for each case as it is finished. You will have an opportunity to discuss the virtues and justice of the different groups' responses.

  a. Bob and Betty Jones are divorcing **amicably** after ten years. He makes $100,000. She is a housewife. There are no children. No one is at fault.

  b. John and Jane Jones (twins of Bob and Betty!) are divorcing after ten years but inamicably. John has been unfaithful. The couple make the same money as Bob and Betty, and **virtually** everything else is the same. Should John pay more than Bob in alimony? How much should he pay?

  c. Anthony and Amanda Jones (actually, there were two sets of triplets, not twins!) are divorcing after ten years, inamicably. Amanda has been unfaithful. Anthony makes the same money as his brothers, and everything else is virtually the same. How much should Anthony pay?

⫸ iBT Preparation

Independent Speaking Task

Students sit in two rows, facing each other. The teacher will read the task. One row will be the speakers, and the other will be the listeners. The speakers will have 15 to 30 seconds (teacher will decide time allotment) to prepare a response of 45 to 60 seconds. When finished, speakers move to the desk immediately to the left and repeat the exercise with a new partner. When speakers have completed the task twice, they become the listeners, so that each student can speak twice. The second time speakers give their response, there will be no preparation time.

Integrated Speaking Task

Read the following passage, and then listen to the passage that the teacher will read. Take notes on both. The teacher will also read a question. You will have 30 seconds to prepare your response. Again, speakers and listeners are in two rows. This time, the speakers respond only once, then roles are switched.

> *Until 2003 couples in China who wanted a divorce needed their work unit's permission, and that was often not given. But in 2003 the rules changed. Now couples can get a divorce from the local community center in ten minutes for about one dollar. The divorce rate has gone up dramatically. The divorce rate more than doubled from 1985 to 1995, and by 2005, the rate had more than tripled, to 1.37 divorces per 1,000 people.*

Rationality (Sunk Costs)

Objectives

- to practice dealing with a concept (rationality) that will play a role in many college courses

- to examine a concept from different points of view—economic, psychological, philosophical

Vocabulary Gloss

freak	= (slang) person obsessed with something
cohesive	= sticking together
vacillating	= changing one's mind often
start from scratch	= start from zero

Introduction

We would all agree that decision making demands rational choice, but what is rational is a subject of much debate, as we shall see as you discuss sunk costs. In fact, *rationality* crosses numerous disciplines and is taught as a course in both psychology and philosophy.

Sunk costs are an investment already made. They can be money, time, emotion, or even lives. Paying attention to these *(honoring sunk costs)* is considered irrational by economists because decisions should be based only on future considerations. But maybe economists don't know as much as they think they do.

For instance (we will talk about this in class as part of our introduction to the subject), do you ever go to a restaurant, eat until you are full, then keep eating *because you paid a lot for it?* You don't want it, but you keep eating it anyway? Many of us have had this experience, and by continuing to eat we are honoring a sunk cost; we are acting irrationally, according to the economists. Whether you eat more or stop eating has no effect on the money you have already spent. That money is gone. So why keep eating?

Another example: You are an astronomy **freak.** Your friend Hank, the artistic director of *Sky and Telescope* magazine, calls and tells you that tomorrow there will be an eclipse of the sun in Bora Bora, and there won't be another for 100 years. Unfortunately, you have bought an unrefundable plane ticket to New York to go to a museum. You would much rather watch the eclipse of the sun, and you won't be able to see it on the plane, but you choose to go to New York because you already paid for the ticket.

This is honoring a sunk cost. Whether you go to New York or not, that money is spent, and it should not be a factor in your decision making—if you want to be rational.

But these examples may not be as clear and simple as they seem. There may be other influences in the decision-making process that are not irrational. For instance if the politicians were thinking of additional jobs that could be created, they would be thinking of the future and not honoring sunk costs. And if you go to New York instead of watching the eclipse because you are worried about losing face with your friends, who would say that you wasted your money, then your decision may not be irrational since losing face is a future consideration.

Similarly, many people defended continuing the Vietnam War because to stop it would have meant that there was no good reason for thousands of deaths that had already occurred. These defenders of the war were honoring a sunk cost. But there were others who wanted to continue the war in order to show the world that we would not abandon other countries when situations became difficult. This second group of people were not making an irrational decision; they were not honoring a sunk cost but thinking of future considerations.

We all like to see our lives as **cohesive.** Most people don't like to cut themselves off from their past. Even if past decisions are foolish ones, people see them as part of their lives, and it is frightening to abandon them because we then face serious questions of identity. The person who chooses to watch the eclipse may be seen by his friends as disordered, unstable, **vacillating,** and unpredictable. These are not positive characteristics, and most people don't like to be perceived in these ways.

So in the final analysis, the economists' notion of rationality may not be the only one. Couldn't we say, for example, that what is rational is what most of the people do most of the time, no matter what that is? At any rate, probably everyone would agree that in order to be rational we must not be contradictory. You should bear this last point in mind as you do the *sunk cost* experiments.

Procedure

Students are assigned to the experiments in pairs. Ask five people (preferably native speakers) your sunk cost question and record their answers. Meet or use the telephone to exchange data. Present the experiment to the class. Your teacher will give each student a photocopy of the *Peer Feedback Sheet* that appears in Unit 6, and the class will rate your presentation. Answer any questions the class has about the experiment. Defend your own opinions and discuss the issue. The presenters should actively participate in the discussion, especially from the point of view of sunk cost. Finally, you will ask for a show of hands for yes or no to the sunk cost question. The second student will write on the chalkboard (1) the results of the original experiment, (2) the results of the ten people asked, and (3) the class's results.

When you present the case to the five people and ask their opinions, try to do as much of it as possible without reading from your books. You don't need to memorize the situation, just present it accurately. Above all, do not let the interviewee read the experiment! This task is designed to make you speak and explain clearly; it is not a reading task for someone else.

Experiment 1

You and your best friend Bob are big football fans, and you spent $100 each for two tickets for the last game of the season, between your favorite team, the New England Patriots, and the New York Jets. On the morning of the game, as you eat breakfast, you watch a snowstorm develop, and the temperature drops to 15 degees Fahrenheit (minus 9 degrees Celsius). Because of new laws against reselling of tickets, you cannot sell the ticket, and it is too late to return it. You and your friend both agree that you would find it more enjoyable to watch the game on TV than to spend several hours in the cold and the snow. Will you go to the game or stay home?

Use this chart to record your results.

Results of 10 People Asked	*Number*	*Percent*
Go to the game	_____	_____%
Stay home	_____	_____%
Class Results	*Number*	*Percent*
	_____	_____%
	_____	_____%

Experiment 2

A few months ago you bought a $100 ticket for a weekend ski trip to Vermont. Several weeks later you bought a $50 ticket for a weekend ski trip to New Hampshire. You think that you will enjoy the New Hampshire ski trip more than the Vermont ski trip. As you put your just-purchased ticket in your wallet, you notice that the Vermont ski trip and the New Hampshire ski trip are both for the weekend that starts tomorrow! It's too late to sell either ticket, and you cannot return either one. You must use one ticket and not the other. Which ski trip will you go on? Why?

The results obtained when this experiment originally was conducted are presented first, followed by a blank chart for you to use in recording your own results.

Which ski trip will you go on?

Original Experiment Results	Number	Percent
$100 ski trip to Vermont	66	54%
$50 ski trip to New Hampshire	56	46%
Results of 10 People Asked	Number	Percent
	_____	_____%
	_____	_____%
Class Results	Number	Percent
	_____	_____%
	_____	_____%

Experiments 2, 3, and 4 were adapted from material created by Hal Arkes and Catherine Blumer in "The Psychology of Sunk Costs," *Organizational Behavior and Human Decision Processes* 35 (1985).

Experiment 3

Students doing this experiment should also read Experiment 4. As the president of Rational Airlines, you have invested $10 million of the company's money in a research project. The purpose was to build a warplane that would not be detected by conventional radar—in other words, a radar-blank plane. When the project is 90 percent completed, another company begins selling a very similar plane that cannot be detected by radar. As far as you can tell, the major differences between your plane and theirs are that their plane is much faster and costs far less to operate than the plane your company is building. The question is, should you invest the last 10 percent of the research funds to build the radar-blank plane, or should you abandon the project?

The results obtained when this experiment originally was conducted are presented first, followed by a blank chart for you to use in recording your own results.

Original Experiment Results	Number	Percent
Yes	82	85%
No	14	15%
Results of 10 People Asked	Number	Percent
Yes	_____	_____%
No	_____	_____%
Class Results	Number	Percent
Yes	_____	_____%
No	_____	_____%

Experiment 4

Students doing this experiment should also read Experiment 3. As president of Trans-Rational Airlines, you have received a suggestion from one of your employees. The suggestion is to use the last $10 million of your research funds to develop a plane that would not be detected by conventional radar, in other words, a radar-blank plane. However, another firm has just begun marketing a plane that cannot be detected by radar. Also, it is apparent that their plane is much faster and far more economical than the plane your company could build. The question is, should you invest the last $10 million of your research funds to build the radar-blank plane proposed by your employee? (*Note:* Here, you **start from scratch,** and the $10 million is the total sum needed to produce the plane.)

The results obtained when this experiment originally was conducted are presented first, followed by a blank chart for you to use in recording your own results.

Original Experiment Results	Number	Percent
Yes	20	17%
No	100	83%
Results of 10 People Asked	Number	Percent
Yes	_____	_____%
No	_____	_____%
Class Results	Number	Percent
Yes	_____	_____%
No	_____	_____%

Experiment 5

You have decided to see a play. The price is $10 per ticket. Standing in the ticket line, you discover that you have lost a $10 bill. Would you still pay $10 for the play? (*Note:* You have enough money to do so.)

The results obtained when this experiment originally was conducted are presented first, followed by a blank chart for you to use in recording your own results.

Original Experiment Results	Number	Percent
Yes	322	88%
No	42	12%
Results of 10 People Asked	Number	Percent
Yes	_____	_____%
No	_____	_____%
Class Results	Number	Percent
Yes	_____	_____%
No	_____	_____%

Experiments 5 and 6 are adapted with permission from Amos Tuersky and Daniel Kahneman, "The Framing of Decisions and The Psychology of Choice," *Science* 211 (January 30, 1981). Copyright 1981 American Association for the Advancement of Science. Reprinted with permission from AAAS.

Experiment 6

You have bought a ticket to a play for $10. The doors open, and everybody starts to enter the theater. You reach into your pocket for the ticket you know you put there, and you can't find it. You search but can't find it anywhere. You have lost the ticket. The seat was not marked, and it is hopeless to think that you will find it. But there are still tickets on sale. Would you pay $10 for another ticket? (You have enough money to do so.)

The results obtained when this experiment originally was conducted are presented first, followed by a blank chart for you to use in recording your own results.

Original Experiment Results	*Number*	*Percent*
Yes	184	46%
No	216	54%
Results of 10 People Asked	*Number*	*Percent*
Yes	_____	_____%
No	_____	_____%
Class Results	*Number*	*Percent*
Yes	_____	_____%
No	_____	_____%

⫸ iBT Preparation

Independent Speaking Task

Students sit in two rows, facing each other. The teacher will read the task. One row will be the speakers, and the other will be the listeners. The speakers will have 15 to 30 seconds (teacher will decide time allotment) to prepare a response of 45 to 60 seconds. When finished, speakers move to the desk immediately to the left and repeat the exercise with a new partner. When speakers have completed the task twice, they become the listeners, so that each student can speak twice. The second time speakers give their response, there will be no preparation time.

Integrated Speaking Task

Read the following passage, and then listen to the passage that the teacher will read. Take notes on both. The teacher will also read a question. You will have 30 seconds to prepare your response. Again, speakers and listeners are in two rows. This time, the speakers respond only once, then roles are switched.

> *According to traditional philosophy that derives from John Stuart Mill, an act is rational to the degree that it maximizes utility—that is, an act is rational to the degree that it benefits the actor. This idea is favored by economists.*

The International View

Do large numbers of people in your country do things that you or others consider irrational?

Can you recall any incident in your life or any governmental decision that illustrates the *sunk cost* phenomenon?

6

Business Negotiation

Freeloaders

Objectives

- to understand more fully the concept of compensation

- to see how different cultures show differences of strictness in regulating social conformity

Introduction

In this section, you will discuss the idea of compensation in a context that might surprise you—lawn care. This issue also is at the heart of the business case that appears in the next section, The Great Bun Caper. Compensation crosses into the realm of philosophy as well. Because compensation should be just, it is a matter of distributive justice. The concept enters into many business practices—for instance, when laying off people.

Vocabulary Gloss

bountiful	= producing a lot of (usually about fruit or crops)
prized	= highly esteemed
gourmets	= people who know and love good food

dummy	= stupid person
lawn	= grassy area (usually mowed)
mowed	= cut (said of grass or lawn)
laissez-faire	= doctrine of letting things alone, not interfering or regulating (borrowed from French)
outraged	= angered and shocked

Procedure

Write and hand in a one-paragraph answer to each of the questions. In small groups, exchange views on each of the questions. When you are finished, the teacher will elicit from the class as a whole what the general opinion seems to be.

1. Mr. Chu has an apple tree. It is a **bountiful** tree. But many of the apples fall over the fence into Mr. King's yard. Can Mr. Chu climb the fence and pick up the apples? Can Mr. King make a pie from the apples even if Mr. Chu shouts, "Give them back!"?

2. As it turns out, these are the best apples in the state. They are **prized** by **gourmets** everywhere, who will pay a lot for Chu Apples. Mr. King, no **dummy,** realizes their value, so he sells the ones that fall into his yard and makes a nice profit. Mr. Chu demands compensation. Should he get it? If so, how much should he get?

Mr. King, no dummy, sells the apples that fall into his yard.

3. The citizens of Eastwick have almost unanimously agreed that everybody must keep his or her **lawn mowed** to a uniform length of three inches. The one exception is Jack. He is an individualist. He dislikes government interference in his affairs. He hates taxes and is always late in paying them. Jack lets his lawn grow untended and wild. The grass is nearly two feet tall. Even Jack thinks it is kind of ugly, but his philosophy is **laissez-faire** in everything. And he just doesn't like anybody telling him what to do.

Walking down the street, however, Jack is impressed at how uniformly beautiful the lawns are. Their beauty makes him smile and feel good. The property value for the whole neighborhood has certainly increased since the neighbors agreed to keep their lawns in perfect shape.

Now the neighbors are suing Jack for compensation. Although Jack has broken no law, the neighbors say he has unfairly profited from their agreement. They say that he is a freeloader.

Should Jack have to pay them compensation?

⏭ iBT Preparation

Independent Speaking Task

Students sit in two rows, facing each other. The teacher will read the task. One row will be the speakers, and the other will be the listeners. The speakers will have 15 to 30 seconds (teacher will decide time allotment) to prepare a response of 45 to 60 seconds. When finished, speakers move to the desk immediately to the left and repeat the exercise with a new partner. When speakers have completed the task twice, they become the listeners, so that each student can speak twice. The second time speakers give their response, there will be no preparation time.

Integrated Speaking Task

Read the following passage, and then listen to the passage that the teacher will read. Take notes on both. The teacher will also read a question. You will have 30 seconds to prepare your response. Again, speakers and listeners are in two rows. This time, the speakers respond only once, then roles are switched.

> *Eminent domain is the name of a concept by which the government exerts its control of all property, even private property. If the government wants to build a highway and your house is in the way, you can be forced to sell it to the government for a fair price. In 2005, the U.S. Supreme Court **outraged** many people by saying it was legal for government to take property from one private owner and transfer it to another private owner if the economic development would help citizens.*

The International View

In your country, are there enforceable standards for property neatness? In other words, are people legally required to keep their property neat?

The Great Bun Caper

Objectives

- to analyze a business problem and to make recommendations for further course of action

- to learn to write a business memo

- to deal with the problem of fair compensation in a profit-oriented environment

- to make difficult but commonsense personnel decisions

- to practice negotiating skills

- to practice presentation skills

- to analyze "the books"

Introduction

This is the first of two business cases dealing with problems within the framework of hamburger franchises. A *franchisee* is a person who pays a yearly sum to the parent company, or *franchisor*, for the right to sell a product. A contract spells out the fine points of the agreement, such as responsibility for paying advertising costs (which is one of the subjects of dispute in these cases).

Vocabulary Gloss

franchises	= independent branches of a company with many stores
team player	= cooperative, not egotistical, person
maverick	= very individualistic person
sponsored	= gave money for an activity in return for publicity
out of my own pocket	= paid for myself

altruistic	= totally concerned with others, not egotistical
civic	= relating to responsibility as a citizen
go 50/50	= divide the cost evenly
backfired	= had the reverse of the desired effect
dropping in on	= visiting, perhaps spontaneously
hordes	= large crowds
windfall	= sudden and unexpected gain
shell out	= reluctantly pay for
to his chagrin	= (his) feeling embarrassed or humiliated
zealousness	= passionate pursuit
mediate	= to reconcile parties in dispute

Procedure

Two students will be assigned to present the case. One will present the facts of the case; the other will present the negotiation game. All students will read each case, but the presenters have the task of knowing all the vocabulary and understanding all facets of the case so that they can answer students' questions on it. The teacher will meet before class with the presenters to answer any questions they might have.

After the game is finished, students will fill out a Peer Feedback Sheet for each presenter. (A reproducible copy of this sheet appears at the end of The Cow Dung Gaffe section in this unit.) These sheets will be collected (unsigned) and given to the presenters. The presenters' homework is to reflect on and analyze the data, then write a short paragraph on the topic What I Can Do to Improve Next Time, summing up the feedback.

Special notes on the objectives and procedure of the game will follow the reading.

The Great Bun Caper

Adams and Banks run Hamburger Heaven (HH) **franchises** in the town of Eastwick. The franchises are a mile apart. The two men do not get along well, as they have very different managerial styles and personalities. Recently, Adams was so upset at Banks that he called the District Representative (DR) to complain:

> The guy (Banks) is not a **team player.** Everyone knows that. I admit he makes a lot of money, a lot more than I do, and that is maybe what HH (Hamburger Heaven) is looking for, but he is a **maverick,** and in the long run I don't think that helps anybody. For example, last year I **sponsored** a Little League baseball team—**out of my own pocket.** It cost me $500, but it is advertising, too. I mean, the team I sponsored won the city championship, and they had their pictures in the paper with Hamburger Heaven uniforms, and everybody ate at my shop after the game. So my sponsorship was not entirely **altruistic.** I got something out of it, but I also did it out of some kind of **civic** spirit. I asked Banks if he wanted to **go 50/50** on the sponsorship, and he rejected the idea. I went ahead with it anyway. He realized just as much profit from the advertising and the good image as I did, but he did not contribute one cent.

Adams is a resourceful and entrepreneurial guy, with a talent for promotion. Some of his ideas have **backfired;** some have been described as crazy by the previous DR. The most disastrous was filling the franchise with balloons with a picture of a burger on them. Kids kept popping the balloons, irritating some of the clients and startling others. Nonetheless, HH has been by and large supportive of local initiative in promotion, especially since the funding comes from the franchisee.

Popular singer James Tyler was a high school friend of Adams. On August 1, Tyler gave a concert on Cape Cod, after which he took a short vacation, **dropping in on** his old friend Adams.

Adams convinced Tyler to give a free promotional concert on the Boy Scout field. Adams paid $500 for a one-time ad on the local radio station telling about the concert.

The concert was well attended, and business for that day was 20 percent higher than normal, due mainly to the **hordes** of hungry people leaving the field by one of the paths that led through Adams's parking lot.

Since Banks's franchise was equidistant from the concert site, he received a similar **windfall,** nearly 20 percent higher sales volume than predicted—for which he contributed nothing. When questioned by DR, Banks replied:

> Adams never asked me for a dime, but if he had, I wouldn't have given him one. **I shell out** 1 percent of my gross revenues to HH for advertising—that is considerably more than what Adams pays because I make a hell of a lot more than he does. Hey, if the wind blows the apples from his tree into my yard, am I forbidden to eat them? The fact is, I don't like James Tyler. His music is lousy, and his politics are worse. He is anti–atomic energy, and that is anti-American as far as I'm concerned. I don't think we want HH associated with that kind of guy.

DR thought about Banks's point of view as he sat down to french fries and a burger with extra cheese. And he had much more to contemplate, for Adams was giving him an additional headache. Anticipating a 30 percent increase in sales for the concert day, Adams had ordered 30 percent more burgers, but when the delivery truck arrived, he realized **to his** great **chagrin** that he had forgotten to order the corresponding increase in buns. Knowing that Banks compulsively overstocked, Adams unloaded from the delivery truck 30 percent more buns than he had ordered, buns which were to have been delivered to Banks.

Adams rationalized that (1) Banks would not be too upset, since he always had a large stock on hand and had probably again ordered more than he needed; (2) his need justified taking matters into his own hands; (3) the net benefit to HH would be greater; (4) if he asked Banks, his unfriendly competitor would certainly refuse; and (5) he would fairly compensate Banks for any loss incurred due to these actions.

After listening to Adams's story, DR called Banks and asked if he had any response to what seemed a well-reasoned action. Banks replied:

> Yeah, I have a couple of things to say to that. First, my oversupply was not sufficient to my demand—Adams was plain wrong about that. Second, it was not just the monetary loss from running out of buns, it was the embarrassment. How would you like to tell a customer that he cannot have a burger because there aren't any buns? And about cooperating? Hey, if you walk through Harvard Square and hear some street musicians you have no obligation to pay them, even if you like the music.

Adams unloaded from the delivery truck
30 percent more buns than he had ordered.

Out of buns, Banks was furious. He called Adams and complained. Adams was apologetic. When his store closed, he went to Banks's franchise and examined the books. Banks admitted that most of the customers who were refused burgers switched their orders to fries, chicken, or other items. A very small number actually walked out. Calculating this, Adams offered what he thought to be fair compensation to Banks.

But DR's further problem was that Banks insisted that HH punish Adams for his theft. On the one hand, it seemed that Adams's actions deserved to be discouraged, for as Banks pointed out, if this became standard practice, chaos would result.

But DR was reluctant to discourage the kind of local creative promotion that Adams had come up with. The Tyler concert would have cost HH more than $20,000.

But despite his **zealousness,** Adams had only averaged about $60,000 per year from his franchise, while Banks had averaged $100,000, with a stronger upward curve in earnings. DR did not want to alienate his best franchisee. And while he was chewing on this problem along with some fries, Sonny Berger, the regional manager, called and asked DR to send him a memo explaining how he (DR) was going to deal with "the great bun caper."

Relevant Data from Banks's Books

	Total Sales	Sales of Items Requiring Buns	Sales of Items without Buns	Drinks
2007 Avg./day	$2,000	$1,200	$400	$400
9/12/07	$2,800	$1,500	$700	$600

[9/12/07 was the date of the concert]

Usage Note

Sales of items without buns means food items such as apple pies, french fries, frozen yogurt, eggs, etc.

Negotiation Game

Objectives

Banks—to obtain the greatest amount of compensation and to convince DR to punish Adams for his theft

Adams—to pay the least amount of compensation

DR—to **mediate** the dispute in a way that makes everybody happy and that will appear to Sonny Berger to be wise and good for business

Procedure

The class will be divided into groups of three, with each student in every group being assigned one of three roles—Adams, Banks, or DR. Based on the case and your analysis of the "Relevant Data from Banks's Books," each player will argue his or her case. You will have a predetermined amount of time (around 20 min.) in which a decision must be made by DR.

Memos

Each player is required to write a one-page (250 words) memo to Sonny Berger. Assume that Berger has been fairly well informed about the facts of the case, so these need not be repeated. The memo will concern the results of the negotiation. One way to organize the memo is to use the following setup: one short paragraph with background and the decision; one paragraph summarizing Adams's arguments; one paragraph summarizing Banks's arguments; one paragraph on how DR decided to mediate; one paragraph appraising DR's decision. (If you are Adams or Banks, bear in mind that DR will probably see your memo and that you must continue working with him in the future.)

Note: Memos, as opposed to reports, are short and to the point, with no rhetorical flourishes. They do not begin with *Dear* and do not have a closing. Follow this form.

Date:
To: Sonny Berger, Regional Mgr., Hamburger Heaven
From: (*Adams,* or *Banks,* or *DR* —then add your own name)
Re: The Great Bun Caper

iBT Preparation

Independent Speaking Task

Students sit in two rows, facing each other. The teacher will read the task. One row will be the speakers, and the other will be the listeners. The speakers will have 15 to 30 seconds (teacher will decide time allotment) to prepare a response of 45 to 60 seconds. When finished, speakers move to the desk immediately to the left and repeat the exercise with a new partner. When speakers have completed the task twice, they become the listeners, so that each student can speak twice. The second time speakers give their response, there will be no preparation time.

Integrated Speaking Task

Read the following passage, and then listen to the passage that the teacher will read. Take notes on both. The teacher will also read a question. You will have 30 seconds to prepare your response. Again, speakers and listeners are in two rows. This time, the speakers respond only once, then roles are switched.

> *Owning a franchise is advertised as a great way to get rich quickly. Franchisees pay a large sum to open a brand name store, and they often work as long as 80 hours a week to succeed. Still, probably about 50 percent of all franchises fail. If you plan to buy a franchise, be careful of companies that open many franchises at once. These companies can become loaded with debt and unable to assist the franchises.*

The International View

Does your country respect mavericks? Do they have a place in your business culture? Or is there only room for team players?

The Cow Dung Gaffe

Objectives

- to deal with a difficult personnel dilemma
- to negotiate from strength
- to practice role playing
- to practice business memo writing
- to practice presentation skills

Vocabulary Gloss

irrepressible	= impossible to restrain or control
gimmick	= clever trick or stratagem
enclave	= small, distinct community
leaflet	= single sheet of paper with writing on it
gaffe	= embarrassing mistake
dung	= excrement
flop	= failure
hottest	= most popular or successful
bottom line	= (accounting) final balance after computing revenues and expenses
gross	= total income before deductions
roll out the carpet	= treat someone's arrival with dignity
kick your butt	= (slang) defeat you badly
dying to	= (an infinitive) desiring strongly
no-win	= having the appearance of doing badly no matter what happens
bluffing	= pretending to be in a strong position
upcoming	= approaching (in time)
carnage	= bloody killing during a battle (primary meaning)

Procedure

Read the case carefully before class. One or two students will be assigned to present the case.

Then you will be assigned a role as Banks or DR and will negotiate for a predetermined time. Your goal is a settlement that is acceptable to both parties and that makes you look good.

After negotiating, you will have to write a one-page memo.

DR will write to Sonny Berger, Regional Manager, defending his actions. He will inform Berger of the outcome and discuss how it evolved. His actions should be justified as rational and as benefitting HH. In other words, he must show that he did the right thing.

Banks will write to Frank Chase, the outgoing president of the American Brotherhood of Independent Franchisees (ABIF). He must justify the outcome as fitting for a future president. In other words, he must make himself look good.

In both cases, you should assume that Berger and Chase are familiar with the background of the incident, so this only needs to be mentioned briefly.

The Cow Dung Gaffe

No sooner had DR sent his memo to Sonny Berger than the **irrepressible** Adams undertook another promotional adventure that would profit him but not Banks. Adams realized that a large portion of the neighborhood just north of his franchise was Hispanic. From his own pocket he paid for some advertising on the local Spanish-language radio station. He had 50 copies of his menu printed up in Spanish and had them distributed by hand in the Hispanic neighborhood. Afterward, his sales increased 5 percent per month, an increase that seemed to Adams attributable only to his advertising. This conclusion was reinforced by his own observations that more Hispanic people were frequenting the restaurant and that there was an increase in applications for employment by Hispanic youths.

The story of Adams's success immediately spread to the other franchises, and among those first to learn of it was Banks. He immediately set about copying Adams's **gimmick.** He realized that the neighborhood to the south of his franchise was densely populated by Vietnamese and Laotian refugees, and it had been for many years a Chinese-American **enclave.** Though he could find no radio station broadcasting in the necessary languages, Banks paid for the same kind of **leaflet** advertising that Adams had done. However, Banks's costs were three times as much, as he had to have menus prepared in three languages. To his chagrin, he found that the translator—a person who was fluent in

Vietnamese and Laotian—made a **gaffe** in Chinese that equated burgers to cow **dung.**

The advertising proved to be a **flop.** Sales, in fact, decreased slightly. Bitter, Banks deducted his personal advertising costs ($900) from the one percent of revenues due the franchisor at the end of the month.

When the franchisor telephoned Banks to ask for payment, Banks refused to pay the $900, adding that he had never liked the idea of paying the franchisor such a large sum of money for advertising, the fruit of which could never be adequately documented—in Banks's opinion.

When DR threatened him with the loss of his franchise, Banks responded:

> Go ahead, fire me. I have the **hottest** franchise in Massachusetts. The **bottom line** is—you'll lose as much as $100,000 **gross** revenues if you replace me. Justify that to Sonny Berger! You know how he loves the bottom line like his mother. Fire me and I'll go to another hamburger chain. With my record, they'll **roll out the carpet** for me. I'll open a franchise across the street from you and **kick your butt,** and you know I can do it. I drove the Pizza House into bankruptcy—remember?

Sonny Berger wasted no time in calling DR, wondering what was going on in Massachusetts and why all of his headaches seemed to come from Eastwick. Adams and the other franchisees were waiting to see the outcome of the confrontation, as they were not happy paying 1 percent advertising to HH either. And Adams was **dying to** do the same thing Banks had done—subtract his out-of-pocket advertising costs from the 1 percent.

It seemed a **no-win** situation to DR. But after some investigation, he found that Banks might just be **bluffing.** He had just bought a $400,000 house and had taken out a 20-year mortgage. Under these circumstances, would he really walk out? And would another hamburger chain really hire a guy who was fired for failing to fulfill his contractual obligations to the franchise?

DR tried to think of options. Was there a way to compromise? A deal he could make so that Banks might save face? This was important since Banks was a candidate for the **upcoming** election of the president of the American Brotherhood of Independent Franchisees (ABIF). The outgoing president, in effect, chose his successor, and Banks had felt he had a good chance at winning. But neither giving in nor getting fired would help his cause.

⫸ iBT Preparation

Independent Speaking Task

Students sit in two rows, facing each other. The teacher will read the task. One row will be the speakers, and the other will be the listeners. The speakers will have 15 to 30 seconds (teacher will decide time allotment) to prepare a response of 45 to 60 seconds. When finished, speakers move to the desk immediately to the left and repeat the exercise with a new partner. When speakers have completed the task twice, they become the listeners, so that each student can speak twice. The second time speakers give their response, there will be no preparation time.

Integrated Speaking Task

Read the following passage, and then listen to the passage that the teacher will read. Take notes on both. The teacher will also read a question. You will have 30 seconds to prepare your response. Again, speakers and listeners are in two rows. This time, the speakers respond only once, then roles are switched.

> *It's very easy for an American company to make mistakes advertising in foreign countries, just as it is for foreign businesses to make mistakes in English. In the window of the Riyadh Supermarket in Saudi Arabia was the sign:* **Fresh Carnage.** *They meant freshly killed meat, of course. Translation results can be funny. For instance, in Italy, Schweppes® translated its ad for its Tonic Water as "Schweppes® Toilet Water."*

The International View

Banks needed to save face. Is losing face a very serious thing in your country?

Peer Feedback Sheet
1 is best; 5 is worst. Circle your response.

---

1. Clarity of content (Was the presentation clear?)

    1   2   3   4   5

2. Eye contact

    1   2   3   4   5

3. Pronunciation

    1   2   3   4   5

4. Pace

    S   S/E   E   E/F   F

    Slow   Excellent   Fast

S/E is somewhere between Slow and Excellent. E/F is somewhere between Excellent and Fast.

Laying Off at the Auto Plant (A Personnel Dilemma)

Objectives

- to examine our criteria for making difficult personnel decisions

- to attempt to solve a very practical business problem as an individual and as a committee member

Introduction

If you attend business school, you will have to explain your business decisions and defend them. In reality, these decisions are tough because they involve employees' well-being. As a member of a committee, you have a voice in the decision-making process and you have the responsibility for the decision. This may be frustrating, but it is a fact of life in a corporation.

Vocabulary Gloss

laid off	= unemployed (not because of poor performance)
(to get) walking papers	= (slang) to lose your job
fainting spells	= periods of falling unconscious
CEO	= chief executive officer (head of the company)

Personnel Dilemma

You are the supervisor of a division of an automobile factory (auto plant). The company is doing badly, and 25 percent of the work force must be **laid off.** Thus, one of the employees in your division must go, and the decision is entirely in your hands. To whom will you hand **walking papers**?

Procedure

You will read the case and make your decision for homework. Then in class you will meet in small groups. Present your decision and give your reasons. You are now the automobile company layoff recommendation committee. Your boss has demanded that you make a group decision today. The majority rules. When done, each group will defend its decision, briefly, to the class as a whole.

	Tom	Dick	Harriet	Rose
Seniority	25 yrs.	5 yrs.	20 yrs.	10 yrs.
Performance	good	excellent	fair/good	good
Wage	$25/hr.	$15/hr.	$20/hr.	$17/hr.
Age	50	24	39	30
Health	high blood pressure	excellent, but calls in sick 3–4 times per month	unexplained **fainting spells**	suffers from depression
Marital Status	divorced	single	divorced	married
Dependents	1 girl in last year of college	0	3 kids, ages 8, 15, 18	1 boy, age 5
Miscellaneous	has filed several complaints about workplace safety	well-liked, captain of work baseball and basketball teams	ex-husband disappeared 5 years ago and pays no child support	niece of the company president

⫸ iBT Preparation

Independent Speaking Task

Students sit in two rows, facing each other. The teacher will read the task. One row will be the speakers, and the other will be the listeners. The speakers will have 15 to 30 seconds (teacher will decide time allotment) to prepare a response of 45 to 60 seconds. When finished, speakers move to the desk immediately to the left and repeat the exercise with a new partner. When speakers have completed the task twice, they become the listeners, so that each student can speak twice. The second time speakers give their response, there will be no preparation time.

Integrated Speaking Task

Read the following passage, and then listen to the passage that the teacher will read. Take notes on both. The teacher will also read a question. You will have 30 seconds to prepare your response. Again, speakers and listeners are in two rows. This time, the speakers respond only once, then roles are switched.

> *Early retirement is offered by many companies and is usually beneficial for both the employee and the company. While the age of retirement varies, it is usually 65. It is often in the interest of companies to have highly paid executives retire so they can hire a replacement at a lower salary. The employee profits by not having to work and presumably by enjoying life. To be eligible for early retirement, most employees must be of a certain age, usually 50-something, and must have worked for the company a certain number of years, usually around ten.*

Writing Assignment

The higher you rise in a career in business, the more you will be making policy decisions.

Situation: You have been asked by the **CEO** of the auto company to create a policy paper on layoffs. Managers throughout the country will use this policy to determine whom to lay off. You must create criteria for laying off. What, for example, is the most crucial factor in the decision: seniority, performance, age? In your speaking exercise you had data for some factors, but you can think of others.

Part 1

Write a policy paper of one to two pages. Remember that you are giving directions to managers here. There should be no description of how difficult a task this is, no sympathy for the managers who find themselves in a difficult situation. You are trying to prevent managers from making bad decisions, based on foolish criteria, the outcome of which will alienate your workers.

Part 2

One student will be chosen as CEO. He or she will not have to write the policy paper. Instead, this student (the CEO) will collect the papers from all the students in the class. (If it is a large class, two CEOs will be chosen.) The CEO will read all the papers, then evaluate them. The CEO will write comments on the papers, praising them for insights and pointing out where the policy might be strengthened. In class, the CEO will single out one or two policy papers that were particularly insightful and explain why they were.

7

Linguistics

You Don't Understand Me

> When men and women agree, it's only in
> their conclusions; their reasons always differ.
>
> —George Santayana

Objectives

- to understand that miscommunication between the sexes comes in part from the fact that men and women speak, in effect, different languages

- to interpret ordinary speech (*reading between the lines*)

Introduction

You will find in college that linguistics intersects with many disciplines. Here, we will see how linguistics intersects with psychology. You will look beneath the surface meaning of the language, which is something you will have to do in studying literature and other subjects.

We often joke that men and women do not speak the same language. But some psychologists and linguists are taking this joke seriously. They say that there exist, in effect, *genderlects*—dialects spoken and understood among men or among women but not between men and women. Of course, men and women in America speak the same language, English, but how each sex, or gender, communicates is more easily understood by others of the same gender.

Though not much research has been done regarding other languages, it is reasonable to suspect that the same phenomenon of misunderstanding between genders occurs everywhere. Think about whether the following scenarios could occur in your country. Think about incidents you have experienced or know about where there was misunderstanding due to this genderlect phenomenon and relate these to your class.

Vocabulary Gloss

bewildered	= confused, puzzled
nibble	= eat a very small bit
nope	= no
wolf down	= eat very rapidly
adultery	= sexual intercourse between a married person and someone other than his or her spouse
eats	= bothers (slang)
fostered	= encouraged the development of

Procedure

Read each exercise, and write your answer to the question. Then discuss your answers as a class. Compare the differences, if any, between men's interpretations and women's.

Exercise 1

Rhett and Carla O'Hara went to a movie, as they often did on Friday nights.

Carla: Do you want to get some popcorn?

Rhett: (truthfully) No.

Driving home after the very long Civil War movie, Carla did not say anything, which was unusual. Rhett knew she was upset, but he couldn't figure out why. "I'll never understand women," he said to himself.

Question: Why was Carla upset? Did she have good reason to be upset?

Answer: _____

_____

_____

Exercise 2

Henry and Cordelia MacDuff were walking home. Cordelia noticed that Henry was limping slightly, and she asked why. He said that he'd hurt his ankle playing volleyball. She asked when it happened, and he said, "About two weeks ago." Cordelia seemed to be irritated. Henry was **bewildered**. What had he done?

Question: Why was Cordelia irritated? Did she have good reason to be irritated?

Answer: _____

_____

_____

Exercise 3

Miranda is frustrated and upset with her husband Prospero. She relates these recent conversations to her therapist, Dr. Joy.

Miranda:	What time is the performance?
Prospero:	You have to be ready by eight-thirty.
Miranda:	How many guests did you invite to our party tonight?
Prospero:	Don't worry. I got enough wine.

Question: Why is Miranda frustrated and upset? Is there anything wrong with Prospero's responses to her questions?

Answer: _____

_____

_____

Exercise 4

Clea and her husband Anthony are about to go to sleep, and she tells him about what has been bothering her.

Clea: I don't know how to get along with my mother. I felt so abandoned as a kid. She worked all the time and never had any time for me. And now she laughs about how busy she was back then and how neglected I must have felt. But I know she feels guilty, and that's why she drinks too much. But I don't know how to talk to her. It makes me feel so sad.

Anthony: Go up there this weekend. Tell her about all those incidents in your childhood that made you feel bad. And suggest that she join Alcoholics Anonymous, to get some help with her drinking.

(Clea rolled away, onto her side, and said no more, but Anthony could tell that she was crying. He didn't understand why she didn't continue the conversation and work out a plan of what to do.)

Question: Why is Anthony bewildered, wondering why Clea is upset with him? He thinks that all he did was to try to help her solve her problem.

Answer: _____

_____

_____

Exercise 5

It was Friday night and the second anniversary of Orson and Marilyn Goode. They decided just to go to the movies, which they both loved doing. Marilyn eats a lot but does not like to admit it.

> Orson: Want any popcorn?
>
> Marilyn: I'm not really hungry.
>
> Orson: I could eat a horse. But I guess I'll settle for a small pop-corn. Want anything to drink?
>
> Marilyn: No. Why don't you get a medium, and I'll just **nibble**?

Orson bought a medium buttered popcorn for $5.00 and was angry about the cost (small—$3.00; large—$6.00). He was hungry, and when he got angry he got hungrier. They sat down, and he began, as Marilyn saw it, wolfing down the popcorn. The movie would not start for another five minutes, and it was half gone. She always waited for the movie to start before she ate any popcorn.

> Marilyn: Do you think we should save some for when the movie starts?
>
> Orson: **Nope.** Want some?

Marilyn shook her head and looked through her bag for a piece of gum. When the movie started, Orson was surprised and upset at how Marilyn seemed to **wolf down** the remaining popcorn. When they left, Marilyn was unusually silent and seemed to Orson to be in a bad mood. So was Orson. They were very disappointed because they wanted this to be a happy occasion.

Question: Why was Marilyn in a bad mood? Should she have been? What about Orson?

Answer: _____

_____

_____

Exercise 6

Rhett and Carla have been seeing a marriage counselor, Dr. Joy. She has told Rhett to be more open about what bothers him, to confront issues rather than to swallow them so that his anger doesn't build internally and then explode over some small issue. It's Friday night, and Rhett proposes that they see a movie, *The Scarlet Pimpernel.*

Carla: What's it about?

Rhett: **Adultery** or prostitution, I think. I'm not sure. I read the book a long time ago, in high school.

Carla: I think I read it, too.

Rhett: Yeah, it was pretty neat. Maybe it was about the French Revolution.

Carla: Do you know what's playing at the Regent?

Rhett: I didn't check.

Carla: Did you know that the Coolidge Corner Cinema is having a French movie festival?

Rhett: Yeah, I think they have it every year. It's kind of an annual thing. The movie starts at 7:00. We can make it if we leave now.

When they get to the movie, *The Scarlet Pimpernel*, Rhett remembers what Dr. Joy said, and he follows her advice.

Rhett: Carla, can I share something with you? One thing that **eats** me is that we always get a medium popcorn, and I don't feel satisfied with half. Or maybe I'm just possessive. I mean, you hold the popcorn on your knee and I have to reach over, and I want to hold it. If I don't, I feel insecure. It's like the TV remote. So, just so you know, I mean, I'm going to buy a small popcorn, for me. You want one?

Carla: No.

Rhett: Sure? Why the sad face? Did I say something wrong?

Carla: Frankly, my dear, you just don't understand!

Question: Why is Carla sad? Did Rhett say something wrong?

Answer: _____

_____

_____

IIII➡ iBT Preparation

Independent Speaking Task

Students sit in two rows, facing each other. The teacher will read the task. One row will be the speakers, and the other will be the listeners. The speakers will have 15 to 30 seconds (teacher will decide time allotment) to prepare a response of 45 to 60 seconds. When finished, speakers move to the desk immediately to the left and repeat the exercise with a new partner. When speakers have completed the task twice, they become the listeners, so that each student can speak twice. The second time speakers give their response, there will be no preparation time.

Integrated Speaking Task

Read the following passage, and then listen to the passage that the teacher will read. Take notes on both. The teacher will also read a question. You will have 30 seconds to prepare your response. Again, speakers and listeners are in two rows. This time, the speakers respond only once, then roles are switched.

> *Some behaviors of boys and girls are determined biologically. Others are **fostered** by society. This latter is often overlooked or underestimated. For instance, in the United States, we tend to dress baby boys in blue and baby girls in pink. We tend to give boys balls and trucks, while we give girls dolls and let them play dress up. We tend to be uncomfortable when girls become tomboys—in other words, dress and act like boys.*

The International View

What differences do you find, if any, between men's and women's conversation in your native language?

Arranging the Marriage of Indira and Raphael (An Indirect Speech Exercise)

Objectives

- to master the sequence of tenses used in indirect speech (this is essential for successful discussion and negotiation)

- to learn about the cross-cultural ideas of a good marriage partner and how marriage might be arranged

Introduction

Students should prepare by thinking about the following questions, which will be discussed in class before doing the activity.

1. Is there a dowry in your country? If so, who pays it, the woman's or man's family?

2. Do marriage customs vary from city to countryside?

3. What are the roles of the man's and the woman's family in a marriage?

4. What are some marriage customs in your country? In the United States, the bride wears "something old, something new, something borrowed, something blue." She throws a bouquet of flowers to the women and a garter to the men; those who catch these should have luck getting married soon. Rice is thrown. Sometimes friends will try to steal the bride's or groom's clothes before they depart for their honeymoon.

5. Are marriages sometimes arranged in your country?

Vocabulary Gloss

dowry = money or goods traditionally given as a condition of marriage, usually from the bride's family to the groom's

caste = rigid class division in society

demeaning = reducing someone to a lower status

Arranging the Marriage of Indira and Raphael

Imagine the following situation, which takes place in a fictional country that we will call Nadur.

Raphael

Raphael is a 35-year-old man who has never married. He has given in to his parents' insistence and has agreed that it is time to find a wife. His parents are very rich, and they demand a substantial **dowry.** He works in the bank owned by his father. His family belongs to the country's highest **caste.**

Indira

Indira is a beautiful 17-year-old girl who is finishing high school. She has gone to private girls' schools all her life. She comes from the caste just below Raphael's. She loves her parents but has talked about running away to become an actress.

Procedure

Form groups representing either Raphael's family or Indira's family. Each family will have one interlocutor, who will practice indirect speech.

Usage Notes

Indirect speech is the reporting of what someone has said. For example,

> *John:* "She is nice."   direct speech
>
> John said that she was nice.   indirect speech

That in indirect speech is often omitted. Notice too that the tense of the verb *to be* backshifts—that is, it changes to a tense further in the past.

Other changes that are essential for this exercise are

> *can*—changes to *could*
>
> *will*—changes to *would*
>
> *must*—changes to *had to*

Useful structures:

> *They said (that)* . . .
>
> *She asked if* . . .
>
> *They asked whether* . . .
>
> *They told me that* . . .

We often ignore the changes made in indirect speech when the time between the speaking and the reporting is very short. For instance,

> *John:* "It is 12:00."   direct speech
>
> a. John *said* that it *was* 12:00.   indirect speech
>
> b. John said that it *is* 12:00.   indirect speech

Item *a* is formally correct. The verb *is* was changed to the simple past tense to agree with *said*, which is in the simple past tense. However, if the reporting is done almost immediately, *b* is acceptable. In fact, most native speakers of English would say *b*. In this exercise, you will try to speak formally, making as many changes as are practical.

It is a custom in Nadur that the families of the man and woman to be wed do not speak directly to each other. So the arranging of this marriage has to be done indirectly.

1. The family of Raphael will meet and invent the details and history of their son (or cousin, etc.). You should include the following.

   a. his educational background

   b. detailed physical description (including flaws—it is said that he is not terribly handsome)

   c. explanation of why he is unmarried at 35

   d. what you want for a dowry

   e. his hobbies, interests, political leanings, habits (good and bad), likes, dislikes

2. The family of Indira will simultaneously meet and invent the details and history of their daughter (or cousin, etc.). You should include the following.

   a. information on her parents and family

   b. detailed physical description

   c. hobbies, interests, political leanings, habits (good and bad), likes, dislikes

   d. her goals in life

   e. what you wish to give as a dowry

3. The teacher will then give each group different rumors about Raphael and Indira. You must investigate these rumors.

4. The interlocutors will just listen in on the first stage of discussion. Then they will relay questions and answers back and forth between the families, who must be at some distance apart. Two interlocutors are necessary so that both families will be constantly busy either answering or asking. Sometimes both interlocutors will be with the same family, but the teacher will speed one along to the other family. The interlocutors must use indirect speech, which the teacher will monitor.

Presentation

The teacher may ask one or more of you to prepare a presentation on wedding customs in your country. Your classmates will have many questions for you, and they may compare or contrast wedding customs in their countries.

IIII➡ iBT Preparation

Independent Speaking Task

Students sit in two rows, facing each other. The teacher will read the task. One row will be the speakers, and the other will be the listeners. The speakers will have 15 to 30 seconds (teacher will decide time allotment) to prepare a response of 45 to 60 seconds. When finished, speakers move to the desk immediately to the left and repeat the exercise with a new partner. When speakers have completed the task twice, they become the listeners, so that each student can speak twice. The second time speakers give their response, there will be no preparation time.

Integrated Speaking Task

Read the following passage, and then listen to the passage that the teacher will read. Take notes on both. The teacher will also read a question. You will have 30 seconds to prepare your response. Again, speakers and listeners are in two rows. This time, the speakers respond only once, then roles are switched.

> *Linguistics and gender intersect in interesting ways. A male is called an* actor; *a female is traditionally called an* actress. *Some women find the latter term **demeaning** and prefer* actor *for both sexes. We have* aviator *(male) and* aviatrix *(female), but the latter term is disappearing. We have* housewife, *but not* househusband *or* housepartner.

The International View

See the five questions in the introduction to this section.

Conditionally Speaking

Objectives

- to understand the larger semantic issues of conditionals

- to see that linguistics can be fun as well as challenging

- to understand speech acts

- to introduce the relation of logic and conditionals

Introduction

As students, you learn rules regarding the use of conditionals, but you normally are not exposed to the debate that goes on in linguistics over basic issues, such as what a conditional is. In this author's view, the jury is still out. Conditionals normally express a relation between two clauses, but just what that relation consists of is not clear. And in fact, a conditional may be expressed with only one clause. You will see also that conditionals may be expressed without an *if*. Dealing with conditionals in this nontraditional way should be interesting and fun. By looking at conditionals in a different way, we may achieve the goal of using them competently and may also have some fun in the process.

> ## Vocabulary Gloss
>
> **donkeys**   = animals similar to horses, with large ears
>
> **stubborn** = not responsive to suggestions

Procedure

Answer as many questions as you can. Some questions require you to write a sentence or two. In small groups, compare your answers and explain your ideas to the other students. One is a matter of life or death!

1. Do these sentences mean the same thing? If not, explain the difference.

    a. If **donkeys** are slow in Spain, Raúl beats them.

    b. If Spanish donkeys are slow, Raúl beats them.

2. Do these sentences mean essentially the same thing? If not, explain the difference.

    a. If donkeys have green eyes, they are **stubborn.**

    b. Donkeys that have green eyes are stubborn.

    c. Donkeys with green eyes are stubborn.

    d. Green-eyed donkeys are stubborn.

3. The following statement is true: Donkeys are stubborn if they have green eyes, and they are stupid if they have brown eyes.
    True or False: Donkeys cannot be stubborn and stupid.

4. Is there a difference between

    a. If you open your refrigerator, it won't explode.

    and

    b. If you open your refrigerator, then it won't explode.

5. The butler doesn't have mud on his shoes. If the butler is the murderer, he left by the window. If he left by the window, he has mud on his shoes. Is the butler the murderer?

6. *Speech Acts and Conditionals*
    Speech acts include offers, promises, denials, rewards or inducements, threats or warnings, appeals or requests. In the following two examples, you will decide what kind of speech acts are being used, and you will decide what the relationship is between the listener and the speaker. This is tricky: There may be more than one answer!

    Note: A C is an average grade, not good and not bad.

    a. "Marry my daughter and I'll give you a C."

    The speaker is a _____ (profession).

    The listener is a (good/bad) _____.

    The speech act is _____.

b. "Marry my daughter or I'll give you a C."

The speaker is a _____ (profession).

The listener is a (good/bad) _____.

The speech act is _____.

c. Task

Many Americans make mistakes using past conditional.

Correct: If I had won the lottery, I would have bought a BMW.

Incorrect: If I would have won the lottery, I would have bought a BMW.

The reason for the error is complex, but it has to do with *I had* and *I would* both being abbreviated to *I'd*.

Write the correct and incorrect sentences above on a piece of paper and ask ten native speakers which is correct or if both are correct. Report your results to the class. The class will then add up all the correct and incorrect answers and figure out what percentage of native speakers make this error.

Alternatively, you could say the sentences and record the results of your survey, instead of showing the written sentences. You could even compare the amount of errors in spoken English as opposed to written English.

⫸ iBT Preparation

Independent Speaking Task

Students sit in two rows, facing each other. The teacher will read the task. One row will be the speakers, and the other will be the listeners. The speakers will have 15 to 30 seconds (teacher will decide time allotment) to prepare a response of 45 to 60 seconds. When finished, speakers move to the desk immediately to the left and repeat the exercise with a new partner. When speakers have completed the task twice, they become the listeners, so that each student can speak twice. The second time speakers give their response, there will be no preparation time.

Integrated Speaking Task

Read the following passage, and then listen to the passage that the teacher will read. Take notes on both. The teacher will also read a question. You will have 30 seconds to prepare your response. Again, speakers and listeners are in two rows. This time, the speakers respond only once, then roles are switched.

> *Philosophers and scientists use conditionals in thought-experiments. Isaac Newton, for example, asked: If a canon ball were shot with high velocity (speed) or low velocity, what kind of orbit would it take? More recently, philosopher John Rawls conducted a thought experiment to help people decide what kind of society rational people would want to live in if they were in what he calls the "original position."*

Presentation

If you are interested in linguistics, you may ask the teacher if you can do a presentation of conditionals in your language, perhaps explaining how they differ from English conditionals.